Tasty Adulting starts by walking you through the foundations of cooking and builds up your kitchen confidence and know-how. Then, 75 fun, quick, and totally doable recipes meet you exactly where you are, allowing you to make mistakes, encouraging you to try new techniques, and gearing you up to reign supreme at the dinner table. With chapters like Souper Heroes, Put Some Meat on Your Bones, and A Sweet Finish, as well as a whole section for having people over, this book helps you move toward that golden "I have my life together" feeling.

And just like that, you're Adulting.

TASTY™
ADULTING

TASTY™

ADULTING

nail it in the kitchen
every mealtime

CONTENTS

INTRODUCTION

What is adulting? Adulting is stepping up to the plate when it matters. But adulting is also phoning it in when you need to. Adulting is enjoying the freedom that comes with independence, and adulting is learning that actions have consequences. Adulting is treating yourself in flush times, nourishing yourself in lean times, and eating cake for breakfast because you can. Adulting is about having fun, living thoughtfully, taking responsibility, making bad decisions, throwing caution to the wind, practicing self-care, and being iconic.

Did you think we were talking about *life*? No, that was about this book. It's called *Adulting*.

Welcome to the essential kitchen guide for the young (or young-at-heart) adult. From breakfast to dinner, dining solo to hosting friends, it's everything you need to know about food that's delicious, interesting, and grown as hell.

How? Well, *Adulting* is like your favorite teacher in high school who gave you serious life lessons, but also let you skip class sometimes. You'll find advice for stocking a pantry with smart ingredients and help in equipping a kitchen that's ready to tackle anything. Plus the recipes are exactly the kind of fun, exciting, tasty (get it?) meals you'll be proud to show off! We'll be there all along the way to offer smart tips to keep you on track, teach you something new, and improve your confidence in the kitchen. Adulthood means learning to let go, take care of yourself, and, well, grow up. Whether you're moving into your first apartment or you've had "get my life together" on your to-do list for years, there is completely necessary advice in this book for you.

HOW TO APPROACH A RECIPE

Read it. No, seriously. Read it all the way through. Then read it again.

Don't skip the headnote or sidebar—these contain important information. We have specifically outlined Life Skills for you throughout this book. These are the technique-driven tips and hacks that we want you to be able to take with you to the next cookbook and the one after that. They're our grown-up gifts to you.

Notice if there are long gaps in active time, like baking or refrigeration. Imagine each step of the process and see if any questions come up for you. Basically, think of a recipe as a map: Look at where you're going and be sure you know how you're getting there. If you're not sure, look it up! There's a time to wing it and a time to learn. Preparation time is about learning.

Now start to gather your ingredients. Check out how they are all prepared, especially if it's in more than one way. Prepare and separate them as instructed. Chop everything so you're not wasting time doing that later (or worse, overcooking one thing while you rush to slice the next thing!). Use a plate, bowls, and/or a cutting board to arrange your ingredients into groups so they'll be together when you need them. Do four dry spices go in the pot at the same time? Premeasure them all into a small bowl so you can accomplish that in a flick of the wrist. Are onions going in right after the butter? Line them up side by side so you can work in order. If there is a long gap in active time, prepare only what you need now. Use the downtime to prepare for the next portion so the ingredients are fresh.

This very adult act of being prepared is called *mise en place*; it's a French term that means "put in place." It might seem like a waste of time to mise en place instead of tackling each step on the fly, but trust us on this one: An organized cook is a relaxed cook. And saying it in French is even more mature.

HOW TO NAIL IT EVERY TIME

This is the fun part. Turn on a playlist you love, crank the volume, and start with step one.

Remember that cooking is not a race. Relax and work with focus. Don't rush to the next step because you think the food is ready or because you're hangry. Confirm that what is supposed to happen *is* actually happening—our recipes will always give you a time range, but we'll also tell you how to know it's working. Use your senses to check in constantly. Are you hearing a sizzle when the chicken breast hits the pan? Do those biscuits look golden brown? Can you smell the spice mix blooming? Does that sautéed bell pepper feel crisp or tender or crisp-tender?

The most important sense of all is the sense of taste. Taste, taste, taste, every step of the way! The number one thing that takes a dish from *wahhh* to *wow* is seasoning well. Keep a small bowl of kosher salt and a pepper grinder within reach. As each component is finished, take a little bite and ask yourself: Does this taste good? If you think so, it seems likely others will, too.

Finally, every pro cook knows that a clean workspace is the best workspace. Move prep bowls or plates to the sink as you empty them (bonus points if you find time to wash them during a pause in active cooking time!), wipe down the counter, clean your cutting board in between uses, and keep your utensils on a rest. Nothing feels better than sitting down to eat with half the dishes already done.

HOW TO NAIL IT WHEN YOU'RE DEFINITELY *NOT* NAILING IT

The most important step in learning to cook is actually cooking. Like any skill, it takes practice, patience, and perseverance. Get in the kitchen and make mistakes! Burn things, oversalt, skip a step, forget to turn the oven on.

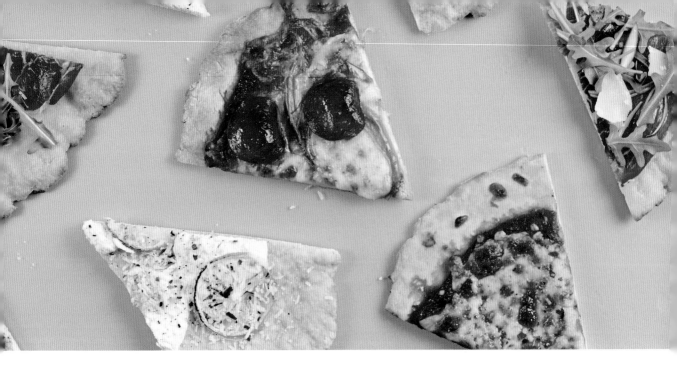

But let each mistake be a lesson on your way to becoming a smarter, more attentive cook.

There's a time to wing it and a time to learn. When things go off the rails, wing it. Check in with your senses and ask what you can do to save this meal. Do you smell something burning? Take it off the stove and reduce the heat before you go to the next step. Was your pinch of salt more like a small handful? See if adding some oil, broth, or water would make sense to regain balance. Is your oven smoking? Open the door, wave a towel to clear the air, and assess the damage.

Smart problem-solving can bring almost anything back from the brink. (And never underestimate a shower of fresh parsley or a squeeze of lemon to cover imperfections!) If it doesn't come out exactly as you'd planned, don't stress. Serve what you can and don't apologize for it. Worst case, you start over. Worst-worst case, you order a pizza. And pizza really isn't all that bad. All that matters is you try again. And again. And again.

HOW TO NAVIGATE THIS BOOK

Take it chapter by chapter and let your stomach decide!

Pasta la Vista will have you executing a noodle night without searching for your rubber frisbee of a jar opener—no, you'll have hot tomato sauce bubbling away *that you made*. Souper Heroes will help you stock your freezer with neatly labeled soups, ready for the day when you *just can't even* and need comfort at your core. Salad Days will up your desk lunch game with colorful concoctions that don't cost $12, entitling you to low-key bragging without having to say a word.

Dive off the deep end with fish, a very adult protein that's quick and adaptable. Or boost your chicken, steak, and pork with exciting new flavors that are as addictive as they are easy. Ditch the processed, packaged faux-meat for whole-food vegetarian (we see

you!) meals that are equally nourishing and exciting.

But *Adulting* is also like, "I'm a cool mom!" so A Balanced Breakfast straddles the line between smart starts to the day and junky ones (that, tbh, are also sort of smart). A Sweet Finish will have you whipping up seriously impressive desserts that look a hundred times harder than they are. And when you are hosting friends—probably the greatest perk of being an adult—Company's Coming is an all-out celebration!

This book will also teach you how you can drag some of your childhood favorites into adulthood with you. Literally, we adulted them. Start your morning with Homemade Breakfast Tarts (see page 24), a delicious sub for your favorite toaster tarts. Your inner six-year-old, who still craves veggies and ranch (everyone's favorite snack), will love Charred Carrots and Broccoli with Ranch Yogurt (see page 58). Things like Spaghetti and Meatballs Done Right (see page 74) and Perfect Roast Chicken (see page 114) are the nostalgic

Sunday supper vibes you need when you're missing home. Distant memories of soggy microwaved fish sticks will be banished forever by Beer-Battered Fish and Rings (see page 94). And having friends over will feel sophisticated AF after you learn A Cheese Plate Done Right (see page 170).

The absolute best part of *Adulting* is owning all of these recipes. Casually mentioning that you have a Seared Tuna Salad (see page 102) or Flourless Chocolate Dream Cake (see page 154) in your back pocket is so grown up. Rolling into a party with a Guacamole Glow Up (see page 175) or gathering your loved ones for Cozy Chicken and Dumplings (see page 122) is unbelievably mature. Pulling a batch of Carrot Cake Muffins (see page 29) out of the oven or Chicken Noodle Soup (see page 42) off the stove is practically Martha Stewart–level. But best of all is diving in, making something great for yourself, and discovering that you had it in you all along.

That, my friend, is peak *Adulting*.

A WELL-STOCKED
KITCHEN

Cheap and Easy

Let's start with the basics. Shop around (or read reviews!) to find the intersection of cheap but well-made tools. Every kitchen should have:

Measuring spoons. Preferably ranging from ¼ teaspoon to 1 tablespoon.

Measuring cups. Preferably ranging from ¼ cup to 1 cup. Dry measuring cups can be used for either dry or wet ingredients. You'll know when it's time to add a liquid measuring cup.

Cutting board. Go big, sturdy, and nonslip. Don't worry about having separate ones for meat, fish, and vegetables—just wash your cutting board well between uses.

Mesh strainer. Get a large one for draining pasta, washing grains, rinsing beans, straining stock, sifting flour, sprinkling powdered sugar, steaming vegetables, catching lemon seeds. The uses are endless.

Wooden spoon. Gentle enough to stir, sturdy enough to smash.

Silicone spatula. Perfect for mixing, folding, scraping, and dividing.

Whisk. One large classic whisk will do everything you need it to.

Silicone tongs. Silicone tips are better than metal for a no-slip grip, plus they won't scratch cookware. Great for everything from flipping meat to lifting cooked spaghetti out of the water to rescuing a stray potato.

Can opener. The classic still works best.

Metal fish spatula. Thinner and sleeker than a standard spatula, the fish spatula can sneak into tight places while still flipping everything from meat to pancakes.

Spider skimmer. Think of this as a slotted spoon, but more efficient. It's essential for frying foods and for small tasks like fishing bay leaves out of the pot.

Ladle. Great for soups, obviously, but also perfect for dividing batter, making pancakes, and drizzling sauces.

Instant-read thermometer. Buy a digital one for quick reads on meat temperatures and checking if your oil is ready for frying.

Rolling pin. Roll out dough, smash cucumbers, tenderize meat, crush ice, grind spices, crumb graham crackers. A single piece of wood makes for the easiest and most versatile roller. (Pro tip: You can use an empty wine bottle in a pinch!)

Grater. Zest citrus, finely grate cheese, process ginger and garlic, grind nutmeg.

Vegetable peeler. Peel apples, make zucchini ribbons, grate big pieces of Parmesan, shave chocolate garnishes. Y-shaped or swivel work about the same, so pick your preference.

Mixing bowls. Find a stackable set of small, medium, and large bowls for easy storage. Stainless steel is the best for easy cleaning and won't hold odors like plastic can.

Oven mitts and trivet. Find a comfortable set of oven mitts and a trivet for hot pots and pans.

Kitchen towels. Decorative tea towels are wonderful. But kitchen towels (more absorbent and eco-friendly than paper towels) are the best for catching spills and cleaning up surfaces. In a pinch, you can use these on a hot surface as well.

Food storage. For packing lunches, storing leftovers, freezing soups. Glass or silicone sets are great, but a cheap, reliable, and eco-friendly move is washing and saving takeout containers. (The round quart-size containers are storage gold.)

Masking tape and permanent marker. Do not rely on your memory! Anything that goes in your fridge or freezer should be immediately labeled with what it is and a

date. (You might want to add your initials, too, in roommate situations.)

Plastic wrap, tinfoil, and parchment paper. For all things storage and baking.

Investment Items

These are the necessities that deserve some investment. Go midrange so you're not breaking the bank, but also not having to replace them every few years. Every kitchen should have:

Chef's knife. This is practically the only knife you need. It doesn't have to be expensive, just make sure it's a comfortable size and weight for you—you'll be using it a lot. A dull knife puts you in danger of slippage and accidents, so also invest in a knife sharpener to keep it in prime shape (or find out where you can have it sharpened).

Serrated knife. A perfect partner to the chef's knife, it's great for slicing through crusty bread and even better for cutting soft tomatoes with ease.

Paring knife. This is much smaller than a chef's knife, ideal for precise tasks, like trimming or making small slices.

Rimmed baking sheet. Find a half sheet pan that's roughly 18 by 13 inches with a 1-inch rim. Go for a thick, sturdy pan that will hold its shape and evenly conduct heat for perfect browning every time.

Large and small saucepans. For basics, from making rice to reheating leftovers.

Nonstick skillet. Great for scrambled eggs, pancakes, fish, anything delicate that shouldn't be heavily seared.

Cast-iron skillet. For getting a hard sear on meats and vegetables, and moving back and forth between the stove and oven. Investing in a good 12-inch skillet (and taking care of it, see note, below) is step one of adulting. If you're ready to do this, then you're ready for plants, a pet, maybe even a baby and a mortgage.

Dutch oven. Use it to make soups, boil pasta, deep-fry, bake bread, braise meat. A 5- or 6-quart capacity will be just right.

Blender and food processor. Plenty of brands make great multiuse blenders with food processor attachments. Save space (and money!) by getting a ninja-like machine that can do both.

9 by 13-inch metal baking pan. Roasting meat, making lasagna, baking a cake, building a casserole. This is a good standard size and you can build a tinfoil wall to create any other sizes you might need.

LIFE SKILL

Cleaning a cast-iron skillet is the most important part of owning one. Use warm water and a pan brush to get the surface clean. Use a mixture of kosher salt and a few drops of oil to scrub off any stuck-on bits. Soap can be your absolute last resort, but never use any abrasive sponges. Place the skillet on a burner over high heat to dry it thoroughly. Remove it from the heat, dab a paper towel with neutral oil, and wipe the entire inside of the skillet to coat. Cool completely before storing.

Optional Upgrades

Do you *need* them? Absolutely not. There are plenty of work-arounds that make all of these tools medium to very optional. But at some point your kitchen routine might become advanced enough that these could be real time-savers.

Grill pan. A cast-iron skillet will give anything a great sear, but if you're craving grill marks—or need a deeper char without overcooking—a grill pan is worth it.

Electric hand mixer. A whisk can do everything a hand mixer can do, but if you often find yourself whipping egg whites or heavy cream or batters, it might be time to give your arm a break.

Muffin tin. There's an easy hack if you don't have one (see page 29). But if muffins and/or cupcakes are in heavy rotation, then get yourself one (or several!) of these.

8 by 8-inch baking pan. Great for making brownies, roasting tomatoes, small-batch enchiladas, or anytime you don't need a full 9 by 13-inch baking pan. Also handy, in some cases, when you don't have other types of specialized pans.

Loaf pan. Use it for baking breads, cakes, meat loaves, small lasagnas, and freezing homemade ice cream.

Cake pan. Cake pans are kind of a single-use item. (Spoiler: It's cake.) Recipes can call for a variety of diameters and heights, so this is an item that you'll likely accumulate over time as needed.

Springform pan. Another single-use item. (Still cake.) But this one covers a wider range of ice cream cakes, tarts, cheesecakes, and buckles, so it's slightly more useful than a standard cake pan.

Deep-dish pie pan. Should every pie be deep dish? Absolutely. Is every pie recipe made for deep dish? No, not often. This is a true special item for the real pie-heads.

Cookie scoop. Also known as an ice cream scoop, this useful tool typically comes in a set of 2-teaspoon, 1½-tablespoon, and 3-tablespoon sizes. Cookie scoops are perfect for portioning out muffins and cookies, dividing cake batter, even scooping the perfect meatball.

A WELL-STOCKED PANTRY

Most of these ingredients can be purchased fairly inexpensively, and with their long shelf lives, you'll have to buy them only on occasion anyway. These are the foundations of most recipes, so keep them around at all times. (A well-stocked pantry is *so* adult.)

Fats

Extra-virgin olive oil. There are some delicious and inexpensive brands of extra-virgin olive oil in every grocery store, perfect for everyday cooking. Keeping a second bottle of more expensive, super-flavorful EVOO for dressings, dips, and finishing dishes is very adult.

Neutral oil. With light flavors and high smoke points, neutral oils are perfect for deep-frying, stir-frying, and high-intensity cooking. Vegetable, canola, and grapeseed oils are all affordable, versatile choices.

Toasted sesame oil. Look for a reasonably-priced bottle of toasted sesame oil for maximum flavor. At high heats, it will turn bitter, so save this for dressing and finishing dishes. (Regular sesame oil—not toasted—is great for cooking!)

Unsalted butter. Stick with unsalted so you can control the salt levels in your food. We think good butter is worth its weight in gold.

Acids

Red wine vinegar. Super flavorful, red wine vinegar adds a lot of punch to any dish. Use it to stand up to (or cut through) big, rich flavors.

White wine vinegar. Good for dressing delicate salads or lighter meats.

Rice vinegar. Rice has a subtle sweetness that pairs well with Asian flavors. Look for unseasoned.

Condiments

Dijon mustard. Forget all other mustards—this is the one. Dressings, sauces, and sandwiches will get a ton of flavor, without an overpowering mustard aftertaste.

Mayonnaise. Mayo is a secret weapon for adding a ton of flavor and holding everything together.

Ketchup. Not just for burgers, ketchup is great for adding savory acidity to sauces and glazes.

Hot sauce. Hot sauce can range from Mexican-style to the ubiquitous sriracha. Pick one that you love for everyday use and grab a couple other styles to meet the needs of specific dishes. (But let's be honest, if you're a Hot Sauce Person, you already have at least six in the fridge.)

Honey. Honey can be expensive, but it's worth it to invest in a good bottle, preferably from somewhere local.

Dry Goods

Pasta. Keep a few boxes of various pastas in your cupboard. Pasta is a fast, cheap, and easy weeknight meal, and a great way to use up produce and proteins you have lying around.

Rice. Similar to pasta, rice can step in for a filling and cheap clean-out-the-fridge meal. Keep a couple varieties of rice, like brown and basmati, on hand at all times.

Anchovies. Think you don't like anchovies? Be an adult and give them one more try. When mixed into a dressing, or melted into oil at the start of a dish, they add a salty, savory flavor that perks everything up. They're one of our favorite pantry tricks.

Bread crumbs. Perfect for binding, coating, and topping, bread crumbs are the triple threat worth keeping around. Buy plain; you can add herbs and spices as needed.

Flour. All-purpose is the standard for most recipes. Any whole-wheat, nut, or cereal flours should be stored in the refrigerator or freezer. They contain high levels of natural oils and will spoil at room temp.

Baking soda and baking powder. Both are leavening agents, but they react differently. Baking soda reacts to acid, so the rise begins immediately. Baking powder reacts to acid and heat, so the reaction starts immediately, but the rise happens in the oven. Note that they cannot be used interchangeably, even though they're often used together.

Granulated sugar. The standard for sweetener. This is the white sugar you're used to seeing.

Brown sugar. Brown sugar is granulated sugar mixed with molasses. Light brown sugar has a more subtle flavor than dark, giving it a higher adaptability and broader application.

Powdered sugar. The perfect finishing touch when breakfast or dessert needs a little something fancy, and essential for glazes and frostings. It's sometimes labeled as icing sugar or confectioners' sugar.

Seasonings

Salt. Kosher salt should be your standard. It's flaky enough to pinch and season with ease, but it isn't as aggressively salty as other types. (Plus it's cheap in bulk!) Also invest in a good flaky sea salt, like Maldon or Jacobsen, for finishing touches on desserts, meats, and vegetables.

Pepper. Buy a sturdy pepper grinder and restock the peppercorns as needed. Nothing beats freshly ground pepper—the oils in the peppercorns activate for an extra pepper-y taste, plus you can control the grind from fine to coarse.

Dried herbs and spices. Dried herbs are much more powerful than fresh, so be careful about substituting one for the other (see note, opposite). Dried spices are best when heat and fat can activate the flavor (known as blooming), so make sure they interact with heat at some point while using them. The dried herbs and spices used in this book are:

dried bay leaves	ground allspice
dried chives	ground cinnamon
dried dill	ground cumin
dried oregano	ground ginger
dried parsley	ground nutmeg
	ground turmeric
caraway seeds	
cumin seeds	Cajun seasoning
fennel seeds	Old Bay seasoning
sesame seeds	red pepper flakes
	smoked paprika
cayenne pepper	
chili powder	vanilla extract
curry powder	
garlic powder	
onion powder	

Build up your spice rack over time to avoid one expensive grocery bill. Keep everything visible and clearly labeled so you can find it. And keep a list on your phone of what you have so you don't end up with six cinnamons.

LIFE SKILL

If you have to swap in dried herbs for fresh ones, reduce the amount by about a third.

Fresh

Meats, produce, herbs, and **dairy** should be purchased as close as possible to the day you'll need them.

Buying **meat** in bulk can be cheaper in the long run, so portion and freeze what you don't immediately need. Just remember to move it to the refrigerator at least twelve hours before you need it so it has time to defrost.

Similarly, frozen **fruit** can be useful in months when it's out of season.

Buying **vegetables** and **herbs** in small quantities may seem tedious, but it's cheaper than throwing them out after a few days. Some frozen vegetables, like peas and corn, are often tastier and easier than buying fresh.

Cheese, milk, and **eggs** should all be bought as needed to prevent spoilage. Shredded cheese can be frozen and thawed later, but everything else should be used before the expiration date.

A BALANCED BREAKFAST

HOMEMADE BREAKFAST TARTS

MAKES 9 TARTS

Even as kids, we knew the "part of a balanced breakfast" moment in the commercial was pure lies. But a day without a gooey pastry straight from the toaster did feel incomplete in an indescribable way. While one part of adulting is making smart choices about your food, the other part is justifying choices with smart logic. Here's an example: When made from scratch—without chemicals and preservatives—are these really any worse than grabbing a pastry from a cafe? See? It's that easy!

FOR THE DOUGH

2½ cups **all-purpose flour**, plus more for dusting

2 teaspoons **granulated sugar**

1 teaspoon **kosher salt**

2 sticks **unsalted butter**, cubed and chilled

¼ cup **ice water**

1 large **egg**

2 teaspoons **milk**

FOR THE FILLING

½ cup (packed) **light brown sugar**

3 teaspoons **all-purpose flour**

2 teaspoons **ground cinnamon**

2 teaspoons **molasses**

FOR THE GLAZE

1½ cups **powdered sugar**

1 teaspoon **ground cinnamon**

½ teaspoon **vanilla extract**

2 or 3 tablespoons **milk**

1 Make the dough: Sift together the flour, sugar, and salt into a medium bowl. Add the butter and use clean hands to squeeze it into the flour until a crumbly, sandy mixture forms with some small chunks of butter A. Add the ice water and swirl with your hands to form a cohesive dough. (If the bowl still has lots of crumbles, add 1 more tablespoon of water.) Divide the dough in half and wrap each half in plastic B. Refrigerate for about 30 minutes.

2 Make the filling: Whisk together the brown sugar, flour, cinnamon, and molasses in a small bowl C.

3 Line a rimmed baking sheet with parchment paper. Remove a ball of dough to a well-floured work surface. Roll the dough into a thin rectangle, about ⅛ inch thick and 10 by 13 inches in size. Use a ruler and knife to mark a 9 by 12-inch work area on the dough and then cut out nine 3 by

4-inch rectangles D . (A pizza cutter makes this a breeze!) Carefully lift the rectangles and lay them on the baking sheet.

4 Whisk together the egg and 2 teaspoons of milk in a small bowl. Brush each dough rectangle with the egg mixture E and lay 1 tablespoon of filling in the centers of the dough pieces F .

5 Remove the other ball of dough from the refrigerator and repeat the cutting process. Lay the new dough rectangles on top of the prepared dough. Gently press the centers of the tarts to flatten the filling, then use a finger to firmly seal the borders. Use the tines of a fork to press the edges together, then use the fork to gently poke rows of holes along the centers of the tarts G . Transfer the baking sheet to the refrigerator to chill for about 30 minutes.

6 Meanwhile, set a rack in the center of the oven and preheat to 350°F.

7 While the oven preheats, make the glaze: Whisk together the powdered sugar, cinnamon, vanilla extract, and 2 tablespoons of milk in a medium bowl to form a gooey glaze that falls off the whisk in a thick stream H . If it seems too stiff, add 1 more tablespoon of milk.

8 Remove the baking sheet from the refrigerator and transfer directly to the oven. Bake for 20 to 22 minutes, turning the baking sheet halfway through, until the tarts are lightly golden all over. Remove from the oven and let the tarts cool on the sheet for about 15 minutes. Spoon a tablespoon of glaze in the center of each tart and gently spread it with the back of the spoon I . Allow the glaze to set for about 5 minutes before eating.

A

B

C

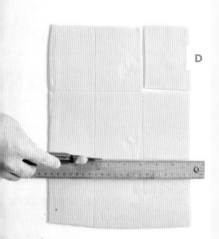

D

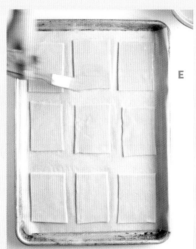

E

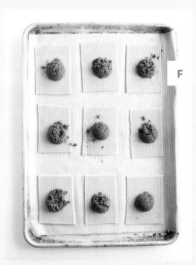

F

G

H

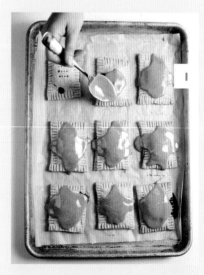

I

carrot cake muffins

Nonstick cooking spray

FOR THE FILLING

1 (8-ounce) package **cream cheese**, at room temperature

¼ cup **granulated sugar**

1 teaspoon **vanilla extract**

FOR THE MUFFINS

1 cup **all-purpose flour**

½ cup **whole-wheat flour**

1 teaspoon **kosher salt**

1 teaspoon **baking powder**

½ teaspoon **baking soda**

½ teaspoon **ground cinnamon**

¼ teaspoon **ground ginger**

1 cup (packed) **light brown sugar**

1½ sticks **unsalted butter**, melted

1 large **egg**

2 tablespoons plain **Greek yogurt**

½ teaspoon **vanilla extract**

1½ cups shredded **carrots**

½ cup **raisins**

½ cup chopped **pecans**

Being an adult means no one is going to stop you from eating cake for breakfast. These muffins sit somewhere in between indulgent and smart. They're stuffed with a sweet cream-cheese frosting, but the batter includes health-forward ingredients like whole-wheat flour, yogurt, carrots, and pecans. So let's just agree that it all evens out in the end. Let them eat cake!

1 Set a rack in the center of the oven and preheat to 425°F. Coat the cups of a standard 12-cup muffin tin with nonstick spray, or use paper muffin liners.

2 Make the filling: Whisk together the cream cheese, sugar, and vanilla in a small bowl until fully combined.

3 Make the muffins: Sift the flours, salt, baking powder, baking soda, cinnamon, and ginger into a medium bowl. In a separate medium bowl, whisk together the sugar, butter, egg, yogurt, and vanilla. Add the flour mixture in thirds, whisking to combine each addition before adding more. Use a spatula to fold in the carrots, raisins, and pecans.

4 Scoop 1½ tablespoons of batter into each muffin cup. Use a wet finger to press the batter across the bottoms of the cups. Scoop 1 tablespoon of filling into the center of each cup. Top the filling with 1½ more tablespoons of batter.

5 Bake the muffins for about 5 minutes, then reduce the oven temperature to 350°F and continue baking for 15 to 18 minutes more, turning halfway through, until the tops are starting to crack and turn golden brown. Let cool completely in the pan.

LIFE SKILL

Don't have a muffin tin? Cut parchment paper and foil into twelve 5 by 5-inch squares. Take a piece of parchment and press it around the bottom of a drinking glass. Press the foil over the parchment to make a solid shape. Place the muffin cup on a rimmed baking sheet. Repeat with the remaining parchment and foil.

glazed berry biscuits

FOR THE BISCUITS

2 cups **all-purpose flour**

⅓ cup **granulated sugar**

2 teaspoons **baking powder**

1 teaspoon **kosher salt**

½ teaspoon **baking soda**

1 stick **unsalted butter**,
cubed and chilled

1 cup **buttermilk**

1 cup **freeze-dried** or
dried blueberries

FOR THE GLAZE

½ cup **powdered sugar**

1 tablespoon **fresh lemon juice**

1 teaspoon **vanilla extract**

A great biscuit recipe is a key part of every adult home. If that recipe happens to include a drizzle of lemony glaze, it just means you're never too old to have fun. These perfectly soft, gently sweet biscuits are at their best when they're still warm. And with a recipe this easy, a new batch can be coming out of the oven every weekend!

1 Set a rack in the center of the oven and preheat to 400°F. Line a rimmed baking sheet with parchment paper.

2 Make the biscuits: Sift the flour, sugar, baking powder, salt, and baking soda into a medium bowl. Add the butter and use clean hands to squeeze it into the flour until a crumbly, sandy mixture forms with some small chunks of butter. Add the buttermilk and swirl the mixture with your hands to form a cohesive, sticky dough. Place the bowl in the freezer to chill for about 15 minutes.

3 Add the blueberries to the bowl and gently fold to incorporate. Use a ¼-cup measure to portion 8 balls of dough onto the baking sheet. Use wet hands to gently flatten and shape the dough into 1-inch-thick discs. Bake for about 15 minutes, until the biscuits are light golden brown. Let cool slightly on the sheet for about 10 minutes.

4 Make the glaze: Whisk together the powdered sugar, lemon juice, and vanilla in a small bowl. Use a spoon to drizzle the glaze over the still-warm biscuits.

LIFE SKILL

Sifting mixes ingredients together in a way that helps break apart any big clumps. Set a fine-mesh strainer over a bowl, add the dry ingredients to the strainer, lift it a few inches above the bowl, and gently tap. If you don't have a mesh strainer, add the ingredients directly to the bowl and use a whisk to mix.

apple pie granola

1½ cups **pitted dates**

1 cup **boiling water**

¼ cup **tahini**

2 teaspoons **ground cinnamon**

¼ teaspoon **ground nutmeg**

¼ teaspoon **ground allspice**

¼ teaspoon **kosher salt**

3 cups **old-fashioned rolled oats**

1 cup **raisins**

½ cup **raw cashews**,
coarsely chopped

½ cup **raw pecans**,
coarsely chopped

½ cup **dried apple**,
cut into ½-inch pieces

¼ cup **raw sunflower seeds**

¼ cup **raw pumpkin seeds**

¼ cup **unsweetened
shredded coconut**

This granola is serious fall vibes. Warm spices wrap themselves around every oat cluster and piece of fruit. It's like eating an apple pie or apple oatmeal or a baked apple, or walking through the woods in your favorite sweater, hearing the leaves crunch under your feet and smelling a fireplace burning somewhere in the distance. Oh, and with zero added sugar and all whole-food ingredients, it's super healthy, too.

1 Set a rack in the center of the oven and preheat to 300°F. Line a rimmed baking sheet with parchment paper.

2 In a food processor, combine the dates and water and soak for about 10 minutes, until soft and pliable. Add the tahini, cinnamon, nutmeg, allspice, and salt and process until smooth.

3 In a large bowl, stir together the oats, raisins, cashews, pecans, apple, sunflower and pumpkin seeds, and coconut. Pour the date mixture over the top and stir to incorporate. Spread the granola evenly onto the baking sheet and bake for about 30 minutes, stirring halfway through, until deeply toasted and very fragrant. Let cool completely and store in an airtight container for up to 2 weeks.

smoky shakshuka
with goat cheese & herbs

2 tablespoons **olive oil**

1 medium **white onion**

4 **garlic cloves**

1 tablespoon **smoked paprika**

1 teaspoon **ground cumin**

¼ teaspoon **red pepper flakes**

1 cup chopped **kale**

1 (28-ounce) can **crushed tomatoes**

Kosher salt and **freshly ground black pepper**

6 large **eggs**

4 ounces **goat cheese**

2 tablespoons finely chopped **fresh cilantro**

2 tablespoons finely chopped **fresh dill**

2 tablespoons finely chopped **fresh mint**

We love going out for brunch as much as anyone, but every bank account has its limits. For the weeks when tax and tip just aren't going to fly, bring the experience to you with a generous skillet full of shakshuka. Pair it with the Herbaceous Salad with Tangy Yogurt Dressing (see page 66) and have your crew bring the crusty bread and bubbly. Voila: Brunch.

1 Heat the oil in a large skillet over medium heat. When the oil is shimmering, add the onion and cook, stirring occasionally, for about 5 minutes, until slightly softened. Add the garlic, paprika, cumin, and red pepper flakes and cook for about 1 more minute, until fragrant. Add the kale and tomatoes and simmer for 10 to 12 minutes, until the kale is wilted and the sauce is thick and bubbling. Season with salt and black pepper.

2 Use a wooden spoon to make 6 small wells in the sauce. Crack 1 egg into a small bowl and then gently pour the egg into 1 well. Repeat with the remaining 5 eggs. Cover the skillet and cook for 7 to 10 minutes, until the whites are just set and the yolks still look soft.

3 Remove the skillet from the heat and dot the sauce with small dollops of goat cheese. Finish with a messy sprinkle of the herbs. Serve the shakshuka directly from the skillet, scooping 1 egg and plenty of sauce onto each plate.

LIFE SKILL

Cracking an egg into a separate bowl may seem like a waste of a bowl, but it gives you a chance to catch any eggshells before they end up in the dish. And, more importantly, it prevents any spoiled eggs from contaminating your food.

frittata for days

Nonstick cooking spray

12 large **eggs**

¼ cup **buttermilk** or **milk**

½ pound **new potatoes** or **creamer potatoes**, cut into ¼-inch-thick rounds

1 tablespoon **olive oil**

Kosher salt and **freshly ground black pepper**

¼ cup finely chopped **white onion**

1 **garlic clove**, minced

½ teaspoon **dried oregano**

½ teaspoon **smoked paprika**

½ cup chopped **kale**

½ pound **pencil asparagus**, cut into 2-inch pieces, or standard **asparagus**, halved lengthwise and cut into 2-inch pieces

½ cup **shredded cheese**, such as **mozzarella**, **cheddar**, **Monterey Jack**, or a **blend**

Easier (and healthier) than starting the day with a greasy egg sandwich, this frittata is great to whip up on Sunday and grab to go all week! Hearty vegetables mix with enough eggs to keep you full and enough spices to keep it interesting. A blanket of cheese bubbles brown on top for the perfect finishing touch. Add this frittata to your meal prep routine, and by Wednesday you'll be thanking yourself.

1 Set a rack in the center of the oven and preheat to 450°F. Coat an 8 by 8-inch pan with nonstick spray.

2 Whisk the eggs and buttermilk in a large bowl until fully combined.

3 Toss the potatoes with the olive oil and a generous amount of salt and pepper in the prepared pan. Bake for about 10 minutes, stirring halfway, until the potatoes are browned and crispy. Stir in the onion and garlic and bake for about 2 minutes more, until fragrant. Stir in the oregano, paprika, and kale to slightly wilt. Add the asparagus and season with another pinch of salt. Pour in the egg mixture and stir to incorporate.

4 Loosely cover the pan with foil and bake for about 25 minutes, until the frittata is puffy and mostly set in the center. Carefully remove the foil and sprinkle the cheese over the top. Bake for 5 to 8 minutes more, until the cheese is melted and just starting to brown.

5 Allow the frittata to cool at least 10 minutes before slicing into 6 equal portions. Store in an airtight container in the refrigerator for up to a week.

freezer-prep
greens & protein smoothie

1 cup **spinach**

1 **banana**, cut into ½-inch pieces

1 **apple**, peeled and cut into
½-inch-thick slices

¼ **cucumber**, cut into
½-inch-thick wheels

1 (1-inch) piece **fresh ginger**,
peeled and halved

¼ cup **all-natural creamy
peanut butter**

1 tablespoon **ground flax**

¼ cup **old-fashioned rolled oats**

1 cup **non-dairy milk**

1 scoop **protein powder,
collagen powder,
or superfood powder**

Get a head start on the day by making breakfast tonight! There is almost nothing more adult than that. Freezing healthy ingredients ensures that their nutrients and flavors stay intact throughout the week, until you're ready to enjoy them. Portioning them makes prep easy—just toss in a blender and go. The mix of sweet and smart here yields a healthy breakfast without it tasting like a chore. We recommend multiplying this recipe to make enough bags to fuel your week.

1 In a half-gallon freezer-safe bag, add the spinach, banana, apple, cucumber, and ginger. Scoop the peanut butter into the center of the bag and cover with the flax and oats to prevent sticking. Press all the air out of the bag and seal. Use a permanent marker to write the date on the bag and freeze for up to 3 months.

2 When ready to use, empty the bag into a blender. Add the milk and protein powder and blend on high until smooth. Pour into a cup or shaker bottle.

LIFE SKILL

The fastest way to peel ginger is with a soup spoon. Turn the bowl of the spoon upside down and use the tip to scrape the skin away.

MAKES 2 SANDWICHES

egg-in-a-hole
croque madame

2 tablespoons **unsalted butter**

1 tablespoon **all-purpose flour**

½ cup **milk**

Pinch of **ground nutmeg**

Kosher salt and **freshly ground black pepper**

1¼ cups shredded **Gruyère cheese**

4 thick slices **bread**

2 large **eggs**

6 thin slices cooked **ham**

¼ teaspoon **smoked paprika**

Madame might have a regal name, but on the inside she's still a hometown gal. Fried in butter with a gooey center of warm ham and melted cheese, a perfectly runny yolk, and an extra blanket of cheese sauce, there is absolutely nothing refined about this sandwich. But what she lacks in class, she makes up for in personality. A breakfast sandwich has never been so saucy.

1 Preheat the broiler to high.

2 Melt 1 tablespoon of butter in a medium saucepan over medium-high heat. Whisk in the flour and cook, stirring occasionally, until golden brown and fragrant, about 2 minutes. Whisk in the milk and bring to a boil. Reduce the heat to medium and simmer, whisking occasionally, for about 3 minutes, until a thick sauce forms. Whisk in the nutmeg, salt, pepper, and ¼ cup of the cheese A . Remove the pan from the heat.

3 Take 2 slices of bread and cut a circle out of the middles, using a small cookie cutter or the rim of a drinking glass B . (Discard the cutouts or reserve them for another use.)

4 Melt the remaining 1 tablespoon of butter in a large oven-safe skillet over medium heat. Crack the eggs into a small bowl. Lay the 2 slices of cutout bread in the skillet and gently pour an egg into each hole. Season the eggs with salt and pepper and cook until the whites have set, 3 to 4 minutes C . Sprinkle the remaining 1 cup of cheese over the bread and eggs and lay 3 slices of ham on each. Gently place the remaining 2 slices of bread on top of each sandwich and flip to toast the new side, about 3 minutes more D .

5 Remove the skillet from the heat. Spoon the cheese sauce over the sandwiches, dividing evenly. Place the skillet under the broiler and cook for 2 to 3 minutes, until the sauce is bubbly and golden in spots. Remove and sprinkle with the paprika to finish. Serve immediately.

SOUPER
HEROES

CHICKEN NOODLE SOUP

SERVES 4

There's a reason chicken soup is nicknamed Jewish penicillin. The simplicity of broth, meat, vegetable, and noodle is like the warmest hug ever. Double or triple this recipe to keep some in the freezer for sick days, bad days, or days you just need a bowl of soup.

4 cups **chicken broth** (see page 46) or store-bought **chicken stock**

1 pound boneless, skinless **chicken breast**

Kosher salt

½ pound wide **egg noodles**

½ pound **carrots**, sliced into ½-inch-thick rounds

¼ cup loosely packed **fresh parsley leaves**

1. Bring the broth to a boil in a large saucepan over high heat. Season both sides of the chicken breast with salt, then add to the boiling broth. Cover and reduce the heat to low. Simmer for about 8 minutes, until the chicken is cooked through. Remove the chicken to a cutting board. Skim away any foam from the top of the broth.

2. Increase the heat to high and return the broth to a boil. Add the noodles. After about 2 minutes, add the carrots. Cook for about 5 minutes more, until the noodles are al dente and the carrots are tender. Reduce the heat to low.

3. Using tongs or two forks, shred the chicken into bite-size pieces. Return the chicken and any collected juices to the broth, along with the parsley. Cook for about 2 minutes to warm the chicken through. Taste for seasoning, then serve immediately. Alternatively, let the soup cool and then transfer to airtight containers to freeze for up to 6 months.

5-minute gazpacho

1 pound **beefsteak tomatoes** or **heirloom tomatoes**, quartered

1 **red bell pepper**, quartered

1 **yellow bell pepper**, quartered

1 large **cucumber**, quartered

1 medium **shallot**, halved

2 **garlic cloves**

1 **jalapeño**, stem removed

½ teaspoon **ground cumin**

¼ cup **red wine vinegar**

2 tablespoons **olive oil**, plus more for drizzling

1 teaspoon **kosher salt**

When we say five minutes, we mean it. A few chops, a couple swirls in the blender, a drizzle of oil on top, and you're done. Part of adulting is putting care into selecting ingredients, because fresh food is delicious food. Peak summer, when it's too hot to cook and the produce is at its best, is the ultimate gazpacho moment.

1 In a blender or food processor, process the tomatoes for about 10 seconds to break down. Add the red bell pepper, yellow bell pepper, cucumber, shallot, garlic, jalapeño, cumin, vinegar, olive oil, and salt and process until smooth, about 2 minutes.

2 Serve immediately, drizzling each bowl of soup with a little more olive oil. Alternatively, refrigerate in an airtight container for up to 1 week.

homemade bone broth

FOR BEEF BROTH

4 pounds **beef bones** with some meat left on them

2 medium **onions**, quartered

4 medium **carrots**, cut into thirds

2 tablespoons **red wine vinegar**

4 **garlic cloves**

10 whole **peppercorns**

6 cups **ice**

FOR CHICKEN BROTH

3 pounds **chicken bones** with some meat left on them

2 medium **onions**, quartered

4 medium **carrots**, cut into thirds

2 tablespoons **white wine vinegar**

4 **garlic cloves**

10 whole **peppercorns**

6 cups **ice**

If childhood is all about wild abandon, adulthood is about saving now for future payoff, such as saving those leftover ribs, wings, and rotisserie bones in the freezer. (Or shortcut: Ask a local butcher if they have any soup bones!) Then get ready for the ultimate cozy weekend project. After simmering away all day, your savings will yield eight cups of rich and flavorful bone broth, a powerhouse of nutrients to soothe your body from the inside out. Welcome to adulthood!

1 Preheat the oven to 450°F.

2 Place the bones in a large stockpot. Cover with warm water, place over high heat, and bring to a boil. Reduce the heat to low and simmer for about 15 minutes, until a thick foam covers the surface.

3 Drain and rinse the bones with cold water. Lay the bones on a rimmed baking sheet and roast for about 30 minutes. Remove from the oven. For the beef bones, toss the onions and carrots in the meat juices and return the sheet to the oven. Roast for about 30 minutes more, until the vegetables are deeply brown. For the chicken bones, toss the onions and carrots in the chicken juices and move on to the next step.

4 Use tongs to return the bones to the stockpot. Pour 1 cup of warm water over the baking sheet and use the tongs to scrape the browned bits from the bottom. Pour the liquid into the stockpot. Add the vinegar, garlic, peppercorns, and enough water to cover. Place the pot over high heat for 15 to 20 minutes, until the liquid boils, then cover. Reduce the heat to low and simmer for at least 12 hours, but preferably 24 hours. Check the pot every 4 to 8 hours to skim off any foam. Add more water as needed to keep the ingredients submerged.

5 Remove the stockpot from the heat. Fill the sink with 2 inches of water and add the ice. Set a large mesh strainer over a large bowl; drape a large tea towel over the strainer. Very slowly pour the broth into the tea towel, letting it drain before adding more. Remove the strainer and discard the bones, vegetables, and peppercorns. Set the bowl in the center of the ice bath and stir the broth for 10 to 15 minutes, until it feels cool to the touch. Let the stock settle for 10 minutes, still in the cold water, then skim any fat from the surface. Pour the broth into airtight containers and store in the refrigerator for 1 week or in the freezer for up to 6 months.

chicken tortilla soup

1 tablespoon **olive oil**

¼ medium **white onion**, finely chopped

1 **garlic clove**, minced

¼ teaspoon **dried oregano**

¼ teaspoon **ground cumin**

¼ teaspoon **chili powder**

Kosher salt and **freshly ground black pepper**

2 cups **chicken broth** (see opposite) or store-bought **chicken stock**

1 boneless, skinless **chicken breast**

¼ cup **diced tomato**

1 (4-ounce) can **diced green chiles**

1 (15.5-ounce) can **black beans**, drained and rinsed

½ cup **frozen corn**

Lime wedges, too many **tortilla strips**, and **fresh cilantro leaves**, for serving

The only thing better than crispy tortilla strips are tortilla strips swimming in broth. The chip floats on the spoon like Rose in *Titanic* and each bite is a joyful burst of savory spice. The chunks of tender chicken and loaded mouthfuls of chiles, beans, and corn are great, too. But for everyone who has side-eyed a stingy tortilla sprinkle, this one's for you.

1 Heat the oil in a medium saucepan over medium heat. When the oil is shimmering, add the onion and cook, stirring occasionally, for about 5 minutes, until the onion starts to soften. Stir in the garlic, oregano, cumin, and chili powder and season with salt and pepper. Cook for about 1 minute, until fragrant.

2 Add the broth, stir, and increase the heat to medium-high. When the broth begins to boil, add the chicken breast, reduce the heat to low, and cover. Cook for 8 to 10 minutes, until the chicken is cooked through. Remove the chicken to a plate to rest.

3 Add the tomato, green chiles, black beans, and corn to the broth. Cook, stirring occasionally, until all the ingredients are heated through, about 5 minutes. Using tongs or two forks, shred the chicken breast and return it to the soup along with any collected juices. Cook for about 5 minutes more to marry the flavors.

4 Divide the soup among bowls, and serve with a squeeze of lime, a handful of tortilla strips, and cilantro.

LIFE SKILL

Poaching means cooking something submerged in a hot liquid. Just remember two things: low and slow. A gentle simmer at low heat will cook your chicken (or fish!) without making it tough. And taking the time to let it slowly poach and then rest for a few minutes will keep it juicy and flavorful.

loaded
baked potato soup

4 medium **Russet potatoes**, cut into ½-inch pieces

2 tablespoons **olive oil**

½ teaspoon **kosher salt**, plus more as needed

4 tablespoons (½ stick) **unsalted butter**

1 medium **yellow onion**, finely chopped

1 **garlic clove**, minced

¼ cup **all-purpose flour**

1½ cups **heavy cream**

2 tablespoons **sour cream**

2 tablespoons grated **Parmesan cheese**

2 cups **vegetable broth**

Freshly ground black pepper

1 tablespoon **dried chives**, plus more for serving

Shredded **cheddar cheese** and chopped **bacon**, for serving

Let's be honest. Baked potatoes are 95 percent about the toppings. So why not drown them in a pot of butter, sour cream, and cheese and top each bowl with bacon and chives? Welcome to baked potato soup, the most reasonable decision you'll make all day.

1 Preheat the oven to 450°F.

2 Toss the potatoes with the olive oil and ½ teaspoon salt on a rimmed baking sheet A . Bake for about 20 minutes, until the potatoes are tender. Remove from the oven and set aside.

3 Melt the butter in a large saucepan over medium heat. Add the onion and cook for about 5 minutes, stirring often, until the onion has softened. Add the garlic and cook for about 1 minute more, until fragrant.

4 Whisk in the flour and cook for about 2 minutes, whisking often, until the flour is golden and cooked B . Whisk in the heavy cream, sour cream, and Parmesan C . Simmer for about 2 minutes, until the mixture thickens. Add the vegetable broth and season with a large pinch of salt, a good amount of pepper, and the chives D . Bring to a boil, then cover and reduce the heat to low. Simmer for about 20 minutes, until the flavors marry.

5 Use a spatula to scrape the potatoes and their oil into the soup. Stir well to combine. Simmer, uncovered, for about 5 minutes more, until the potatoes are warmed through.

6 Divide the soup into bowls and garnish with cheese, bacon, and more dried chives.

corn chowder
with chorizo

1 tablespoon **olive oil**

6 ounces **chorizo**, casings removed

1 medium **yellow onion**, finely chopped

2 cups **frozen corn**, thawed

Kosher salt and **freshly ground black pepper**

2 cups **whole milk**

2 cups **heavy cream**

Corn and chorizo don't seem like obvious bowl-fellows, but trust us. The spice and richness of the meat plays perfectly off the inherent sweetness of the corn. And has anything ever been more beautiful than bright orange chorizo-infused oil drizzled over the surface of creamy chowder? Impressive and easy, it's the best pairing we've heard of since, well, corn and chorizo.

1 Heat the oil in a medium saucepan over medium heat. When the oil is shimmering, add the chorizo and cook, stirring occasionally, for about 10 minutes, until cooked through. Remove the chorizo and its oil to a bowl and set aside.

2 Add the onion to the saucepan along with 2 tablespoons of water and cook, stirring occasionally, for about 5 minutes, until the onion is softened. Reserve 4 tablespoons of the corn and set aside. Add the remaining 1¾ cups of corn to the saucepan along with another 2 tablespoons of water. Season with salt and pepper. Cook, stirring often, for about 3 minutes, until the corn is tender. Remove the saucepan from the heat.

3 Pour the corn and onion into a blender. Add the milk and cream. Pulse about 4 times to break up the corn into small pieces. Pour half of the chowder back into the saucepan. Process the rest of the chowder until smooth. Stir it into the saucepan and return to medium heat. Simmer for about 10 minutes, until the chowder is thick and warmed through.

4 Portion the chorizo meat among four bowls and pour the soup over the top, dividing evenly. Sprinkle each bowl with 1 tablespoon of the reserved corn and drizzle with chorizo oil.

coconut curry lentil soup

2 tablespoons **olive oil**

1 medium **onion**, finely chopped

2 **garlic cloves**, minced

2 teaspoons minced **fresh ginger**

1 tablespoon **curry powder**

½ cup **brown** or **green lentils**, rinsed and dried

3 cups **vegetable broth**

Kosher salt and **freshly ground black pepper**

1 (13.5-ounce) can full-fat **coconut milk**, well shaken

Fresh cilantro leaves and **lime** wedges, for serving

Warm, comforting, and 1,000 percent feel-good. That sentence was re: the cost of ingredients, but it totally applies to this soup, too. Lentils were kind of like the ramen noodle packs before there was packaged ramen—meaning people with little made lots with a simple ingredient. Boiled in a big pot of densely flavored broth, lentils become a hearty, nourishing, and very satisfying meal. Scraping by never tasted so good!

1 Heat the oil in a medium saucepan over medium heat. When the oil is shimmering, add the onion and cook, stirring often, for about 5 minutes, until the onion is softened. Add the garlic and cook for about 1 minute, until fragrant. Add the ginger and curry and cook for 1 minute more, until the curry is toasted.

2 Add the lentils and stir to coat in the seasonings. Add the vegetable broth and season with a big pinch of salt and good amount of pepper. Bring to a boil, then reduce the heat to medium-low and simmer for about 20 minutes, stirring occasionally, until the lentils are cooked. Remove the pan from the heat.

3 Reserve 4 tablespoons of coconut milk, then add the remainder to the soup and stir to combine. Taste and add more salt and pepper as needed.

4 Divide the soup among four bowls and drizzle each with 1 tablespoon of reserved coconut milk. Top with cilantro leaves and serve with a lime wedge.

bean & beer chili

2 tablespoons **olive oil**

1 large **white onion**, finely chopped

1 **garlic clove**, minced

1 **jalapeño**, minced

1 tablespoon **ground cumin**

1 tablespoon **smoked paprika**

1 tablespoon **chili powder**

2 teaspoons **kosher salt**

2 teaspoons **freshly ground black pepper**

1 pound **ground beef**, 80% lean

1 cup **beef broth** (see page 46) or store-bought **beef stock**

1 (15.5-ounce) can **kidney beans**, drained and rinsed

1 (15.5-ounce) can **chickpeas**, drained and rinsed

1 (15.5-ounce) can **black beans**, drained and rinsed

1 (14.5-ounce) can **diced tomatoes**

2 cups **stout beer**

Shredded **cheddar cheese**, **sour cream**, and **chopped fresh chives**, for serving

Haters will say chili doesn't have beans. While it's true that a pot of all-meat chili is incredible after simmering away all day, time and budget often get in the way. Enter beans. They make a hearty pot that's quickly thrown together, easy on the wallet, packed with protein, and popping with textural variety. It will definitely win any weeknight cook-off contest.

1 Heat the oil in a large saucepan over medium heat. When the oil is shimmering, add the onion. Cook, stirring occasionally, for about 5 minutes, until the onion has softened. Add the garlic, jalapeño, cumin, paprika, chili powder, salt, and pepper. Cook for about 1 minute more, until the spices are toasted and fragrant.

2 Add the beef and use a wooden spoon to break it up into small pieces and incorporate it with the spice mixture. Cook the beef in a single layer for about 5 minutes, until the bottom is browned. Add the broth and use the wooden spoon to scrape up any browned bits from the bottom of the pan.

3 Add the kidney beans, chickpeas, and black beans along with the tomatoes and the beer. Stir everything together and bring to a boil. Cover and reduce the heat to medium-low. Simmer the chili for about 30 minutes, until it has thickened slightly and the flavors have married.

4 Scoop the chili into bowls and top with cheddar, sour cream, and chives.

SALAD

DAYS

CHARRED CARROTS & BROCCOLI WITH RANCH YOGURT

SERVES 2 TO 4

Veggies dipped in ranch dressing are literally heaven on earth. But after a certain age, in polite society, some pleasures need to be kept private. On the other hand—life hack alert!—anything plated beautifully immediately looks adult. This recipe is a way to low-key broadcast your love of ranch while still looking extremely classy.

FOR THE VEGETABLES
1½ pounds **rainbow carrots**

1 (1-pound) head **broccoli**

2 tablespoons **olive oil**

½ teaspoon **kosher salt**

FOR THE YOGURT
1½ cups plain **Greek yogurt**

1 teaspoon **dried chives**

1 teaspoon **dried parsley**

1 teaspoon **dried dill**

1 teaspoon **onion powder**

1 teaspoon **garlic powder**

1 teaspoon **kosher salt**

½ teaspoon **freshly ground black pepper**

1 Preheat the oven to 450°F.

2 Make the vegetables: Scrub the carrots and dry thoroughly. Slice the carrots in half lengthwise to make long strips. Cut the broccoli, including the stem, into long strips. Use a vegetable peeler to remove the tough outer layer of stem.

3 Toss the carrots and broccoli with the olive oil and salt on a rimmed baking sheet. Bake for about 20 minutes, until the vegetables are tender and nicely charred.

4 Meanwhile, make the yogurt: Whisk together the yogurt, chives, parsley, dill, onion powder, garlic powder, salt, and pepper in a small bowl.

5 To serve as a passed side dish, scoop and swoop all of the yogurt onto a large serving platter and lay the vegetables over the top. To serve as a starter salad, swoop a large spoonful of yogurt onto each plate and portion out the vegetables on top.

LIFE SKILL

The scoop and swoop is an essential plating move. Use a large spoon to place a big scoop of your sauce, mash, or soft base in the center of a plate. Place the spoon in the center of the sauce at a 45-degree angle, then swoop the spoon to the edge of the plate, leaving a beautiful trail behind.

SERVES 2 TO 4

dressed-up
avocado salad

FOR THE SALAD

1 (15.5-ounce) can **chickpeas**, drained and rinsed

1 tablespoon **olive oil**

¼ teaspoon **kosher salt**

¼ medium **red onion**, thinly sliced

¼ cup **red wine vinegar**

2 heads **romaine hearts**, root end removed, halved, and leaves separated

1 pint **cherry tomatoes**, halved

2 **avocados**, halved, pitted, and sliced

8 ounces **feta cheese**, cubed

FOR THE DRESSING

5 tablespoons **olive oil**

1 tablespoon **Dijon mustard**

½ teaspoon **dried oregano**

½ teaspoon **kosher salt**

Oven-baked chickpeas are the crispy little champions of any salad, adding a delightfully savory crunch. Then this salad gets all dressed up with a quick-pickled onion, bursting cherry tomatoes, creamy avocados, salty feta, plus a *homemade* dressing that adds a perfect amount of acidity. (What's more grown up than DIY-ing your dressing?) It's like a bang-pow-boom of textures and flavors!

1 Preheat the oven to 450°F.

2 Make the salad: Pat the chickpeas dry with paper towels. Toss them with the olive oil and salt on a rimmed baking sheet. Bake for about 20 minutes, until browned and crisp. Remove from the oven and set aside.

3 Meanwhile, toss the onion and vinegar in a small bowl. Set aside to pickle.

4 Make the dressing: Whisk the olive oil, mustard, oregano, and salt together in another small bowl.

5 Spread the romaine leaves on a large serving plate. Scatter the tomatoes, avocados, feta, marinated onion, and crispy chickpeas on top. Drizzle the dressing all over the salad and serve immediately.

LIFE SKILL

Combining just about anything with acid makes it pickled, like the onion and vinegar here. The long version is to boil and jar in a brine. But the quick version, the acid soak, is pretty good, too—just 15 to 30 minutes in any type of vinegar, lemon juice, or lime juice is the fast-track to a perfect burst of flavor. Try it with thin slices of shallot, cucumber, carrot, or radish next.

SERVES 2

rye bread panzanella

½ cup **olive oil**

2 (1-inch-thick) slices **rye bread**,
cut into 1-inch cubes

3 medium **heirloom tomatoes**,
cut into 1-inch cubes

Flaky sea salt

1 small **shallot**, minced

1 **garlic clove**, minced

¼ teaspoon **cumin seeds**

¼ teaspoon **caraway seeds**

¼ teaspoon **fennel seeds**

½ cup loosely packed **fresh
basil leaves**

¼ cup loosely packed **fresh
parsley leaves**

1 tablespoon **red wine vinegar**

Freshly ground black pepper

Panzanella, an Italian bread salad, traditionally uses stale bread. It's very adult to use up everything available, but you know what's better than stale bread? Fried bread. Crispy little croutons, fragrant with olive oil, soaked in fresh tomato juices. The assertive flavor of rye bread, plus some toasted spices to magnify everything great, turns up the volume. It's a foolproof salad that tastes way more complex than it is.

1 Heat the oil in a large skillet over medium-high heat. When the oil is shimmering, add the bread in one even layer. Fry for about 2 minutes on one side, until golden and crisp. Flip the croutons and fry for 2 minutes more on the opposite side. Transfer the croutons, leaving the oil in the skillet, to a large serving bowl. Add the tomatoes to the bowl and season generously with salt.

2 Return the skillet to low heat. Add the shallot, garlic, cumin, caraway, and fennel. Toast for about 1 minute, until fragrant. Remove the skillet from the heat and pour the mixture over the bread and tomatoes. Add the basil, parsley, vinegar, and a generous amount of pepper. Toss well and serve.

chicken caesar cobb salad

FOR THE DRESSING

½ cup plain **Greek yogurt**

¼ cup grated **Parmesan cheese**

4 **anchovy fillets**, finely chopped

1 **garlic clove**, grated

1 tablespoon **fresh lemon juice**

2 teaspoons **Dijon mustard**

½ teaspoon **kosher salt**

½ teaspoon **freshly ground black pepper**

FOR THE SALAD

4 cups **ice water**

2 large **eggs**

2 thick-cut slices **bacon**

½ pound boneless, skinless **chicken breast**

Kosher salt

3 cups **baby kale**

1 **beefsteak tomato**, diced

1 **avocado**, halved, pitted, and diced

Freshly ground black pepper

2 ounces **Parmesan cheese**

LIFE SKILL

Boiling eggs is as easy as . . . boiling water (and adding eggs). Seven minutes will get you a perfectly set but still-gooey yolk (10 minutes will fully set the yolk). Don't skip this step: Plunging the eggs into ice water stops the cooking *and* makes peeling a whole lot easier.

Caesar salad is delicious, but tbh, it's also pretty sad when you really think about it. Bland romaine, some sprinkles of Parmesan, a couple rock-hard croutons. Depressing! It pales in comparison to its older sister the Cobb, which is the braggy overachiever—chicken! bacon! eggs! Why not take the best parts of a Caesar—the dressing and the cheese—and fuse it with a Cobb, the salad that has something for everyone?

1 Make the dressing: Whisk together the yogurt, Parmesan, anchovies, garlic, lemon juice, mustard, salt, and pepper in a small bowl.

2 Make the salad: Fill a medium bowl with the ice water. Bring a medium saucepan of water to a boil over high heat. Gently lower the eggs into the water and boil for 7 minutes. Immediately transfer the eggs to the ice water and let cool for about 5 minutes. Gently tap the eggshells and peel. Rinse under cold water.

3 Heat a medium skillet over medium-low heat. Lay the bacon in the skillet and cook for 8 to 10 minutes, flipping occasionally, until browned and crisp. Remove the bacon to paper towels to drain.

4 Increase the heat to medium-high. Season the chicken on both sides with salt and add to the bacon fat. Cook for about 9 minutes, until the bottom is nicely browned. Flip the chicken and cook for 6 to 8 minutes more, until cooked through. Remove the chicken to a cutting board.

5 Spread the kale on a large serving plate. Arrange the tomato and avocado in even rows on each end. Slice the eggs in half and arrange in a row down the center. Chop the bacon into large pieces and arrange in a row on one side of the eggs. Slice the chicken and arrange in a row on the other side of the eggs. Generously season the salad with pepper. Spoon the dressing over the salad. Use a vegetable peeler to shave large pieces of Parmesan all over the salad. Serve immediately.

smashed
cucumber salad

2 medium **English cucumbers**

1 tablespoon finely chopped **red onion**

1 tablespoon **sesame seeds**

1 teaspoon **sugar**

1 teaspoon **soy sauce**

1 teaspoon **rice vinegar**

½ teaspoon **toasted sesame oil**

½ teaspoon **kosher salt**

½ teaspoon **red pepper flakes**

Smashing cucumbers breaks open their barriers and allows so much flavor to soak in. And because cucumbers are 95 percent water (for real), flavor in means liquid out. So the longer this salad sits, the more delicious it gets, as flavors mingle, intensify, and pool in the container. It's especially excellent alongside hearty, spicy dishes like the Gochujang and Sesame Skirt Steak (see page 120) to offer something bright.

1 Place the cucumbers on a cutting board. Using a rolling pin, firmly bash the cucumbers in several places, then cut into bite-size pieces, and transfer to a serving bowl.

2 Whisk together the onion, sesame seeds, sugar, soy sauce, rice vinegar, sesame oil, salt, and red pepper flakes in a small bowl to make the dressing. Drizzle the dressing over the cucumbers, then toss to coat.

3 Let the cucumbers marinate for at least 15 minutes before serving. Alternatively, transfer the salad to an airtight container and marinate in the refrigerator for up to 12 hours.

sour cream & onion
potato salad

½ cup plus 2 tablespoons **olive oil**

1 medium **yellow onion**, halved and thinly sliced

Kosher salt and **freshly ground black pepper**

1 **garlic clove**

1 pound **new potatoes** or **creamer potatoes**, halved

½ cup **sour cream**

2 teaspoons **Dijon mustard**

2 teaspoons **onion powder**

1 bunch of **fresh chives**, thinly sliced

1 small **shallot**, thinly sliced into rings

Creamy caramelized onion and crispy fried shallot make this salad fall somewhere in the Venn diagram of onion dip, potato salad, and sour cream and onion chips. Basically, it's a lot of flavors you already love all in one bowl.

1   Heat 2 tablespoons of the oil in a medium skillet over medium heat. When the oil is shimmering, add the onion and season with a generous pinch of salt and lots of black pepper. Cook the onion for 30 to 40 minutes, stirring often with a wooden spoon and scraping up any browned bits on the bottom of the pan, until it is deeply golden and jammy. Add small splashes of water here and there as needed if the pan is getting too dry, and reduce the heat to medium-low if the onion is browning too quickly.

2   Grate the garlic clove into the finished onion, stir to incorporate, and set aside.

3   Meanwhile, bring a large pot of salted water to a boil over high heat. Add the potatoes and cook for 10 to 15 minutes, until a knife easily slides into the center of the largest potato. Drain the potatoes.

4   Return the potatoes to the pot and toss with the sour cream, mustard, onion powder, half of the chives, and the caramelized onion. Set aside to marinate.

5   In a small saucepan, add the remaining ½ cup of olive oil and the shallot. Place the saucepan over medium-low heat to warm the oil and shallot together, stirring occasionally to separate the rings. Cook for 15 to 20 minutes, stirring occasionally, until the rings are golden brown and crisp. Using a spider or a slotted spoon, scoop them out and transfer to paper towels to drain. Immediately sprinkle lightly with salt.

6   Transfer the potato salad to a serving bowl. Top with the fried shallot and the remaining chives.

PASTA

LA VISTA

ADULTED

SPAGHETTI & MEATBALLS DONE RIGHT 74

ULTIMATE HOMEMADE PESTO 78

CACIO E PEPE 79

CHICKEN ZITI AL LIMONE 80

RICOTTA DUMPLINGS WITH BROWN BUTTER & SAGE 81

ZOODLE SHRIMP SCAMPI 84

VEGETABLE OVERLOAD PASTA SALAD 87

COLD SOBA NOODLES WITH PEANUT SRIRACHA SAUCE 88

BAKED BUCATINI PIE 91

SPAGHETTI & MEATBALLS DONE RIGHT

SERVES 4

Grandmothers everywhere will have you believe that meatballs and red sauce are complicated, mysterious things that must be coaxed from the heavens with love by wrinkled hands. But in reality, a simple formula does the trick: (great ingredients + care) x patience = incredible food. That's right—with this equation, you, too, can have perfect meatballs. Take your time, enjoy the journey, taste as you go. That's what adulting is all about—and it's all you need for a perfect platter of Sunday Supper.

FOR THE SAUCE

1 (28-ounce) can **whole peeled tomatoes**

¼ cup **olive oil**

4 **garlic cloves**, smashed

1 sprig **fresh basil**

Kosher salt and **freshly ground black pepper**

FOR THE MEATBALLS

2 slices **white bread**, crusts trimmed

½ cup **buttermilk**

¼ cup grated **Parmesan cheese**

¼ cup **fresh parsley leaves**

1 **garlic clove**

2 large **egg yolks**

1 teaspoon **kosher salt**

½ teaspoon **freshly ground black pepper**

½ teaspoon **dried oregano**

½ teaspoon **ground nutmeg**

½ teaspoon **ground cumin**

½ teaspoon **smoked paprika**

¼ teaspoon **red pepper flakes**

1 pound **ground beef**, 80% lean

2 tablespoons **olive oil**

FOR THE SPAGHETTI

1 tablespoon **kosher salt**

1 (1-pound) box dry **spaghetti**

½ cup grated **Parmesan cheese**

1 sprig **fresh basil**

1 Make the sauce: Pour the tomatoes and their juices into a large bowl. Use clean hands to gently squeeze the tomatoes between your fingers, breaking them into irregular pieces **A**.

2 Combine the crushed tomatoes and juices, oil, garlic, basil, and a generous amount of salt and black pepper in a large saucepan over medium heat. Bring to a boil and simmer, stirring occasionally, for 15 minutes, until the sauce has slightly thickened **B**. Taste and add more salt and black pepper as needed. Pour the sauce back into the large bowl, discard the basil sprig, and wipe out the saucepan.

3 Make the meatballs: Add the bread and buttermilk to a food processor. Soak for about 5 minutes, until the bread is softened. Add the Parmesan, parsley, garlic, egg yolks, salt, black pepper, oregano, nutmeg, cumin, paprika, and red pepper flakes and process until smooth **C**. In a large bowl, add the beef and the mixture from the food processor. Use clean hands to fully combine, but be careful not to overmix.

Divide the meat mixture in half, and then in half again. Divide and roll each section of meat mixture into 2 separate meatballs, creating 8 total **D**.

4 Heat the olive oil in the saucepan from the sauce over medium-high heat. When the oil is shimmering, add the meatballs and fry, turning often, for about 10 minutes, until they are browned all over **E**.

5 Pour the sauce back into the saucepan. Reduce the heat to medium-low. Use a wooden spoon to scrape up any browned bits from the bottom of the pan. Simmer the sauce and meatballs together **F**, turning the meatballs occasionally, while the spaghetti cooks.

6 Make the spaghetti: Bring 3 quarts of water to a boil in a large pot over high heat. Add the salt and spaghetti. Cook to al dente according to the package instructions. Drain the spaghetti and lay it out on a large serving platter. Scoop the meatballs on top and then spoon the tomato sauce over everything. Finish with the Parmesan and sprig of basil.

LIFE SKILL

Al dente is an Italian phrase that means "to the tooth." In plain English, it means cook your pasta long enough to still have a nice firmness, but not so long that it's mushy. That's good pasta.

ultimate homemade pesto

⅓ cup **pine nuts**

2 **garlic cloves**

¾ cup **olive oil**

½ cup grated **Parmesan cheese**

1 teaspoon **kosher salt**

4 cups loosely packed **fresh basil leaves**

Is there anything pesto can't do? From dressing up roasted vegetables to elevating seared meats to being the best dip ever for crusty bread, it's the superhero sauce that won't quit. But we all know its greatest act of heroism is pasta. Literally any noodle is delicious when slicked in the green stuff. Keep a batch in the freezer for those moments when it's dinner time and all hope seems lost. Pesto is the perfect trick to have up your sleeve, and an excellent building block to lots of delicious meals.

1 Heat a small skillet over medium heat. Add the pine nuts and garlic, stirring occasionally, and toast for about 3 minutes, until the nuts are slightly golden and the garlic is fragrant. Transfer to a food processor.

2 Add the olive oil, Parmesan, and salt to the food processor. Process until a smooth paste forms, about 1 minute. Scrape down the sides and add the basil. Pulse in about 6 quick bursts to finely chop the basil.

3 Store the finished pesto in an airtight container for up to 1 week in the refrigerator. Alternatively, freeze the pesto in an ice cube tray, transfer the cubes to a freezer bag, and freeze for up to 6 months. (Use about 4 cubes for 1 pound of dry pasta, or 1 cube per single serving of cooked pasta.)

cacio e pepe

1 tablespoon **kosher salt**

½ pound dry **spaghetti**

½ tablespoon **freshly ground black pepper**

4 tablespoons (½ stick) **unsalted butter**

⅔ cup shredded **Parmesan cheese**

Cacio e pepe literally means "cheese and pepper" in Italian. And that's all there is to this dish. Well, also butter, salt, and spaghetti. Oh, and water. But that's it! Everything you need is probably already sitting in the pantry and fridge. The time commitment is a mere few minutes longer than it takes to boil water. The deliciousness is insane. Do you really need more reasons? Get cooking!

1 Bring 3 quarts of water to a boil in a large pot. Add the salt and spaghetti, stirring to incorporate. Cook the spaghetti for 2 minutes less than the package directions indicate for al dente. Reserve 1 cup of pasta cooking water, then drain.

2 Heat a large skillet over medium heat. Add the pepper and cook, stirring, for about 1 minute, until toasted and fragrant. Add the butter and melt, stirring to coat the pepper.

3 Add ½ cup of the reserved pasta water to the skillet and bring to a simmer. Add the spaghetti and use tongs to toss and coat the pasta with the butter mixture. Reduce the heat to medium-low and add half of the Parmesan. Stir with the tongs, turning the spaghetti occasionally, 1 to 2 minutes, until a thick sauce begins to form. Add the remainder of the Parmesan and continue to stir and turn. If the sauce becomes too thick, add a little more of the reserved pasta water as needed. Taste the spaghetti for doneness and serve as soon as it's al dente.

chicken ziti al limone

FOR THE CHICKEN

1 tablespoon **olive oil**

1 pound boneless, skinless **chicken breast**, cut into 1-inch pieces

Kosher salt and **freshly ground black pepper**

1 cup chopped **kale**

FOR THE ZITI

1 tablespoon **kosher salt**

1 (1-pound) box dry **ziti**

¼ cup **heavy cream**

2 **garlic cloves**, grated or minced

Zest and juice of 1 **lemon**

4 tablespoons (½ stick) **unsalted butter**

½ cup grated **Parmesan cheese**

LIFE SKILL

True, it seems weird to add water to a sauce, but pasta cooking water is heavily salted and loaded with starch from the pasta itself, both of which help thicken the sauce, make it silky, and make your dish well-seasoned.

If you've never had an *al limone* pasta, first: Where have you been?! But also: Get ready! Traditionally a simple buttery, lemony spaghetti dish, our recipe (mostly) throws the rules out the window, using ziti and adding kale and chicken. Everything gets tossed in a creamy sauce exploding with lemony flavor. Maximum deliciousness in every bite!

1 Heat the oil in a large skillet over medium-high heat. When the oil is shimmering, add the chicken and season with salt and pepper. Cook for 6 to 8 minutes, flipping occasionally, until the chicken is cooked through. Add the kale and another pinch of salt and cook for about 2 minutes, until the kale has begun to wilt. Remove to a plate.

2 Bring 3 quarts of water to a boil in a large pot over high heat. Add 1 tablespoon of salt and the ziti. Cook the ziti according to the package directions for al dente, but pull it off the stove 2 minutes before instructed. Reserve 1 cup of pasta cooking water, then drain the ziti and set aside.

3 Return the skillet from the chicken to medium-low heat. Add the cream, garlic, lemon zest, and a pinch of salt. Whisk until it comes to a steady simmer, about 2 minutes. Add the butter, 1 tablespoon at a time, whisking after each addition to melt before adding the next. The sauce will become thicker and creamier with each addition.

4 Add the chicken, kale, and ziti to the skillet and toss to coat. Add ½ cup of the reserved pasta cooking water and the Parmesan. Shake the skillet to swirl the sauce together and toss the ingredients so everything is well coated. Add the remaining pasta cooking water a little bit at a time as needed to fully coat the mixture. Remove from the heat and stir in the lemon juice. Serve immediately.

ricotta dumplings
with brown butter & sage

1 large **egg**

1 cup **ricotta cheese**

¼ cup grated **Parmesan cheese**

¼ teaspoon **ground nutmeg**

1 tablespoon plus ¾ teaspoon **kosher salt**

1 cup **all-purpose flour**, plus more for dusting

4 tablespoons (½ stick) **unsalted butter**

8 **fresh sage leaves**

Puffy, delicate, and soaked in nutty browned butter, these dumplings are like a plate of ravioli that ran away and left their stuffing behind. It takes quick, careful hands to form the dumplings, but otherwise they're a breeze to throw together for a quick weeknight meal (with leftovers!).

1 Whisk together the egg, ricotta, Parmesan, nutmeg, and ¼ teaspoon of salt in a medium bowl. Slowly add the flour A, whisking until just incorporated B.

2 Lightly flour a rimmed baking sheet. Use a soup spoon to scoop out a ball of dough, then use wet hands to shape it into a ball C. Place the dumpling on the floured baking sheet. Repeat with the rest of the dough, until you have about 16 dumplings, spacing them apart. Lightly dust the tops of the dumplings with more flour.

3 Bring 3 quarts of water and 1 tablespoon of salt to a boil in a large pot over high heat.

4 Meanwhile, melt the butter in a large skillet over medium-low heat. Cook, stirring often, for 5 to 6 minutes, until the foam begins to subside and the butter has some golden brown specks D. Add the sage and remaining ½ teaspoon of salt E. Remove the pan from the heat.

5 Use a spider or slotted spoon to carefully place the dumplings in the boiling water F. Simmer, stirring occasionally, for about 5 minutes, until they're cooked through.

6 Use a spider or a slotted spoon to transfer the dumplings to the skillet. Return to medium heat and toss the dumplings to coat in the butter.

7 Divide the dumplings among four plates and spoon the brown butter and sage leaves over the top.

zoodle shrimp scampi

1 pound **large shrimp**, peeled and deveined

2 tablespoons **olive oil**

3 **garlic cloves**, thinly sliced

1 teaspoon **kosher salt**

½ teaspoon **freshly ground black pepper**

¼ teaspoon **red pepper flakes**

1 pound **zucchini noodles**

Juice of 1 **lemon**

4 tablespoons (½ stick) **unsalted butter**

2 tablespoons chopped **fresh parsley**

It's embarrassing to admit, but sometimes—rarely! almost never!—you just can't stomach another carb. Part of being a grown-up is knowing your limits, we guess. Enter zoodles, a not-even-close but whoa-these-are-delicious substitute for pasta. Zoodles—zucchini shredded into noodles—are available in most grocery stores in the produce section or frozen food aisle. Especially when mingling with a lemony sauce and perfectly pink shrimp, zoodles make you feel like you had a salad for dinner, when you actually had pasta. (OK, but you actually had a salad.)

1 Place the shrimp in a large bowl. Add 1 tablespoon of olive oil, the garlic, salt, black pepper, and red pepper flakes and toss to coat. Cover with plastic and marinate at room temperature for 30 minutes, or in the refrigerator for up to an hour.

2 Meanwhile, heat the remaining 1 tablespoon of olive oil in a large skillet over medium heat. When the oil is shimmering, add the zoodles and toss to coat. Cook for 2 to 3 minutes, until the zoodles are tender but still al dente. Transfer the zoodles to a mesh strainer to drain. Wipe out the skillet.

3 Return the skillet to medium-high heat. Carefully pour the shrimp and marinade into the skillet. Cook the shrimp for about 2 minutes, turning once, until light pink. Using tongs, remove the shrimp to a clean plate. Continue to cook the garlic for about 1 minute more, until it just starts to take on color. Add the lemon juice and butter and swirl the pan. Continue to cook and swirl until the butter is melted and the sauce has thickened, about 4 minutes.

4 Add the zoodles and toss to coat in butter sauce. Return the shrimp and any juices back to the skillet. Toss and cook for about 2 minutes more, until the shrimp are just opaque and everything is coated in sauce. Remove the skillet from the heat and sprinkle the parsley over the top. Serve immediately.

vegetable overload
pasta salad

1 medium **red onion**, finely chopped

1 pint **cherry tomatoes**, halved

1 head **broccoli**, cut into small florets

½ cup plus 2 tablespoons **olive oil**

1 tablespoon plus ½ teaspoon **kosher salt**

¼ teaspoon **freshly ground black pepper**

1 (1-pound) box dry **fusilli**

1 cup **frozen peas**

4 **scallions**, thinly sliced

1 **yellow bell pepper**, diced

½ cup loosely packed **fresh mint leaves**

½ cup loosely packed **fresh basil leaves**

Zest and juice of 1 **lemon**

2 **garlic cloves**, minced

¼ cup **red wine vinegar**

1 teaspoon **red pepper flakes**

Memories of bad pasta salads include pungent red onion stealing all the attention, flavorless tomatoes taking up space, and mayonnaise sitting out for a suspiciously long time. In this improved—adulted—pasta salad, soaked onion learns to be a team player, roasted tomatoes earn their spot with addictive bites of concentrated flavor, and a warm garlicky vinaigrette blankets everything in a taste that won't turn on you. (In fact, it only improves as it sits!)

1 Preheat the oven to 450°F. Fill a small bowl with cold water and add the onion. Set aside to soak.

2 Add the cherry tomatoes, broccoli, 2 tablespoons of olive oil, ½ teaspoon of salt, and the black pepper to a large bowl. Toss to combine and spread everything in an even layer on a rimmed baking sheet. Roast for about 20 minutes, tossing halfway, until the tomatoes are blistered and the broccoli is tender. Transfer the vegetables and juices back to the large bowl.

3 Meanwhile, bring 3 quarts of water to a boil in a large pot over high heat. Add 1 tablespoon of salt and the fusilli. Cook to al dente according to the package instructions. Add the frozen peas during the last minute of cooking. Drain the pasta and peas and rinse under cold water to stop the cooking. Add to the bowl with the tomato and broccoli mixture.

4 Drain the onion. Add it to the bowl, along with the scallions, bell pepper, mint, basil, and lemon zest and juice. Season generously with salt and black pepper and toss to incorporate.

5 In a small saucepan, add the remaining ½ cup oil and the garlic. Place the saucepan over low heat until the garlic starts to sizzle, 2 to 3 minutes. Whisk in the red wine vinegar, red pepper flakes, and a generous amount of salt and black pepper. Remove the pan from the heat and immediately drizzle the dressing over the pasta salad. Toss to coat everything well. Marinate at room temperature for at least 30 minutes, and up to 2 hours, before serving.

6 Alternatively, refrigerate the salad for up to 2 days and let sit at room temperature for 30 minutes before serving.

cold soba noodles
with peanut sriracha sauce

1 (3- to 4-ounce) bundle dry **soba noodles**

¼ cup full-fat **coconut milk**, well shaken

¼ cup **all-natural creamy peanut butter**

1 tablespoon **sriracha**

½ tablespoon **toasted sesame oil**

½ teaspoon **kosher salt**

1 **scallion**, thinly sliced

This deeply satisfying dish comes together with just a couple flicks of the wrist. The smooth and slightly spicy peanut sauce could theoretically play with whatever you have lying around: ramen, udon, even spaghetti. But it's best when tossed with the springy density and rich flavor of soba. Pair it with the Smashed Cucumber Salad (see page 70) for a light and healthy meal that is ready in a flash.

1 Cook the soba noodles according to the package directions.

2 Whisk together the coconut milk, peanut butter, sriracha, sesame oil, salt, and 1 tablespoon of water in a medium bowl. Add the noodles and toss to coat.

3 Divide the noodles between two bowls and top with the scallion.

baked bucatini pie

1 tablespoon plus 1 teaspoon **kosher salt**

1 (1-pound) box dry **bucatini**

1 (28-ounce) can **diced tomatoes**

2 tablespoons **olive oil**

5 **garlic cloves**, thinly sliced

¼ teaspoon **red pepper flakes**

10 **fresh basil leaves**, coarsely chopped

½ teaspoon **dried oregano**

2 large **eggs**

1 cup grated **Parmesan cheese**

1 cup grated **mozzarella cheese**

½ cup **ricotta cheese**

Freshly ground black pepper

Can't get enough long, stringy noodles? Do you also love lasagna? Do you never want to have to choose again? Same. This pasta pie hits all the red sauce extravaganza, cheese celebration, and carb overload pleasure centers at once. Like a bowl of pasta, it's great right away. Like lasagna, it's even better as leftovers. You really *can* have it all.

1 Preheat the oven to 400°F.

2 Bring 3 quarts of water to a boil in a large pot over high heat. Add 1 tablespoon of salt and the bucatini, stirring to incorporate. Cook the bucatini for 4 minutes less than the package directions indicate for al dente, then drain.

3 Combine the tomatoes, olive oil, garlic, 1 teaspoon of salt, the red pepper flakes, half of the basil, and the oregano in a large saucepan over medium heat. Bring to a simmer and cook, stirring occasionally, for 20 minutes, until reduced to about 3 cups.

4 In a large bowl, whisk together the eggs, ½ cup of Parmesan, ½ cup of mozzarella, the ricotta, and plenty of black pepper. Add the bucatini and, using tongs, toss to combine. Reserve 1 cup of the tomato sauce and add the remainder to the bucatini. Toss again and then transfer the mixture to a 12-inch cast-iron skillet. Pour the reserved tomato sauce over the top.

5 Bake for about 20 minutes, until the sauce is dark red and the bucatini is crisp on top. Remove the skillet from the oven and immediately sprinkle the remaining ½ cup of Parmesan, ½ cup of mozzarella, and remaining basil over the top. Let the pie cool for 10 minutes before slicing.

LIFE SKILL

Long strands of noodles are pretty much always interchangeable. We love bucatini in this recipe, but spaghetti or capellini would work just as well. Better yet, use whatever you have on hand and be the ingredient-swapping ninja we know you can be!

ONE
FISH
TWO FISH

BEER-BATTERED FISH & RINGS

SERVES 2 TO 4

Forget chips. Fish and rings, both fried in the same beer batter, is the new normal. (Batter efficiency is very adult.) A quick deep-fry puffs the batter to its crispy extreme, while the onion becomes meltingly soft and the fish hits peak flaky. You'll faintly remember your old life with soggy fish sticks and greasy fries, and then realize how great eating grown-up food really is. Serve the fish and rings as they're ready, or transfer to a 200°F oven to keep warm before serving.

FOR THE FISH AND RINGS

1½ pounds **cod**, cut into 1½-inch by 4-inch strips

2 tablespoons **Old Bay seasoning**

2 medium **yellow onions**, sliced into ½-inch-thick rings and separated

FOR THE BATTER

1½ cups **all-purpose flour**

¼ cup **cornstarch**

1 tablespoon **baking powder**

½ teaspoon **kosher salt**

¼ teaspoon **freshly ground black pepper**

2 cups **lager beer**, such as Budweiser or Narragansett

2 tablespoons **malt vinegar**

2½ quarts **vegetable oil**

1 Make the fish and rings: In a medium bowl, toss the fish with 1 tablespoon of Old Bay to fully coat. In a separate medium bowl, toss the onion rings with the remaining 1 tablespoon of Old Bay to fully coat A .

2 Make the batter: Whisk together the flour, cornstarch, baking powder, salt, and pepper in a large bowl. Add the beer and malt vinegar and whisk until smooth B .

3 Heat the oil in a large Dutch oven or saucepan over medium-high heat. Use an instant-read thermometer to check periodically until the oil hits 350°F.

4 Use tongs to transfer a few pieces of fish and onion to the batter C . Turn to fully coat and then remove, allowing excess batter to drip off. Lower each piece into the heated oil. Fry, turning once, for about 5 minutes total, until golden brown. Transfer to a wire rack or paper towels to drain D .

5 Working in batches, batter and fry the remaining fish and rings. Between batches, use a small spoon or spider to remove any stray pieces of batter from the surface of the oil, and allow the oil to return to 350°F.

salsa verde scallops

FOR THE SALSA

Zest and juice of 1 **lemon**

½ cup **fresh parsley leaves**, finely chopped

½ cup **fresh cilantro leaves**, finely chopped

2 **scallions**, thinly sliced

1 medium **shallot**, finely chopped

2 **garlic cloves**, grated

1 teaspoon **kosher salt**

½ teaspoon **freshly ground black pepper**

¼ teaspoon **red pepper flakes**

½ cup **olive oil**

FOR THE SCALLOPS

½ pound **dry sea scallops**

Kosher salt

2 tablespoons **olive oil**

Scallops seem like an impossible headache, when in reality, they're impossibly simple. There are just two unbreakable rules for perfect scallops. First, buy only dry scallops. Wet scallops are packed in water and preservatives to extend shelf life—you'll be buying all that water weight just to have scallop soup when they hit the pan. Dry scallops are guaranteed fresh and will sear beautifully. Second, don't overcook them. Under five minutes will be more than enough. Prep this quick salsa verde ahead of time, throw together the Rye Bread Panzanella (see page 62), and have a spectacular dinner on the table in no time flat.

1 Make the salsa: Whisk the lemon zest and juice, parsley, cilantro, scallions, shallot, garlic, salt, black pepper, red pepper flakes, and ½ cup olive oil together in a medium bowl. Transfer to a small serving bowl.

2 Make the scallops: Use paper towels to pat the scallops dry, then season them with salt. Heat the oil in a large skillet over medium-high heat. When the oil is shimmering, add the scallops, flat side down. Cook without moving for about 3 minutes, until the bottom is golden brown. Use tongs to flip, and cook for 1 to 2 minutes more, until the scallops are solid white on the outside, but still have some give when you press on them.

3 Transfer the scallops to a serving plate and drizzle half of the salsa verde over the top. Serve with the remaining salsa verde alongside.

lowcountry
shrimp & grits

FOR THE GRITS

1 cup **yellow grits**

1 cup shredded **sharp cheddar cheese**

¼ cup **milk**

2 tablespoons **unsalted butter**

¼ teaspoon **kosher salt**

½ cup **frozen corn**, thawed

FOR THE SHRIMP

¼ cup **olive oil**

2 **garlic cloves**, thinly sliced

1 pound **jumbo shrimp**, peeled and deveined

Kosher salt and **freshly ground black pepper**

½ teaspoon **dried oregano**

½ teaspoon **smoked paprika**

Hot sauce, for serving

When things are called lowcountry, you know they're going to be high flavor. These grits have the special joy of two delicious corn textures in one: creamy, cheesy grits and sweet, firm kernels. The shrimp get tossed in a fragrant bath of garlic, oregano, and paprika for tons of savory flavor. And for the true lowcountry experience, keep a bottle of hot sauce within reach.

1 Make the grits: Bring 3 cups of water to a boil in a medium saucepan over medium-high heat. Slowly whisk in the grits. Return to a boil, then reduce the heat to medium-low. Continue whisking the grits periodically for about 20 minutes, until they're creamy but still slightly firm. Add the cheese, milk, butter, and salt and whisk to combine. Reserve 2 tablespoons of the corn and mix the remainder into the grits. Reduce the heat to low to keep warm.

2 Make the shrimp: Heat the oil and garlic in a large skillet over medium heat. When the garlic is sizzling, add the shrimp and toss to coat with oil. Season generously with salt and pepper. Cook for 3 to 4 minutes, turning the shrimp halfway, until just opaque. Remove from the heat and stir in the oregano and paprika.

3 Divide the grits among four bowls. Top with the shrimp and drizzle with the cooking oil from the skillet. Finish with the reserved corn and hot sauce.

chili-lime baked tilapia
with avocado crema

FOR THE TILAPIA

1 pound **tilapia fillets**

1 tablespoon **chili powder**

1 teaspoon **ground cumin**

½ teaspoon **kosher salt**

½ teaspoon **freshly ground black pepper**

¼ teaspoon **cayenne pepper**

Juice of 1 **lime**

1 tablespoon **olive oil**

FOR THE CREMA

1 **avocado**, halved, pitted, and sliced

½ cup **fresh cilantro leaves**

½ teaspoon **kosher salt**

½ teaspoon **freshly ground black pepper**

Juice of 1 **lime**

¼ cup plain **Greek yogurt**

Tilapia gets a bad rap sometimes, but its neutral taste is an incredible asset when it comes to exploring flavors. (And its wallet-friendly price doesn't hurt, either.) An assertive spice rub makes every bite a surprise, and a tangy avocado crema balances the heat. Pair it with the Herbaceous Salad with Tangy Yogurt Dressing (see page 66) for an easy weeknight meal.

1 Set a rack in the center of the oven and preheat to 400°F. Line a rimmed baking sheet with parchment paper.

2 Make the tilapia: Lay the fillets on the baking sheet. In a small bowl, mix together the chili powder, cumin, salt, pepper, cayenne, lime, and olive oil. Use a brush to coat each side of the tilapia fillets with the marinade. Bake the fish for 12 minutes, until the edges begin to crisp and the flesh is moist and flaky.

3 Meanwhile, make the crema: In a blender or food processor, combine the avocado, cilantro, salt, pepper, lime juice, and yogurt. Blend until completely smooth, 1 to 2 minutes.

4 Scoop and swoop the crema onto a serving plate (see page 59). Add the tilapia and serve immediately.

sweet & spicy salmon
sheet pan

2 tablespoons (packed) **light brown sugar**

¼ teaspoon **red pepper flakes**

1 **yellow squash**, thinly sliced

2 ears of **corn**, husked and cut in half

1 **red bell pepper**, cut into strips

½ pound **asparagus**, cut into 1-inch pieces

4 (4- to 6-ounce) skin-on **salmon fillets**

3 tablespoons **olive oil**

Kosher salt and **freshly ground black pepper**

You probably already know this, but sweet and spicy are a match made in heaven. A more unexpected pairing: sweet and spicy *salmon*! The three components play incredibly well together for a glaze that balances perfectly with the fish's subtle-yet-rich flavors. With an abundance of fresh veggies, this meal is an easy one with plenty of leftovers. Feel free to use up whatever is in your CSA, or whatever you find at the farmers' market!

1 Set a rack in the center of the oven and preheat to 425°F. Line a rimmed baking sheet with parchment paper.

2 In a small bowl, whisk together the brown sugar and red pepper flakes with 1 tablespoon of water.

3 Arrange the squash, corn, bell pepper, asparagus, and salmon on the baking sheet. Drizzle with the olive oil, salt, and pepper, and turn the vegetables and salmon to coat. Place the salmon skin-side down in the center of the sheet. Line up the corn in a long row along one edge of the sheet. Spread a mixture of squash, bell pepper, and asparagus on either side of the salmon in an even layer. Spoon about half of the brown sugar mixture over the salmon fillets.

4 Bake for about 15 minutes, until the salmon is opaque and the vegetables are tender. Remove the baking sheet from the oven and spoon the remaining brown sugar mixture over the salmon. Divide the fish and vegetables among four plates and serve.

LIFE SKILL

If you have doubts about finding fresh salmon, frozen is an excellent option. Just remember to move it to the refrigerator at least 24 hours or up to 3 days before you need it. And whether buying fresh or frozen, make sure the salmon skin is descaled!

pineapple fried rice

4 tablespoons **vegetable oil**

2 large **eggs**, beaten

½ pound **jumbo shrimp**, peeled and deveined

3 **garlic cloves**, minced

¼ teaspoon **red pepper flakes**

1 medium **white onion**, finely chopped

2 cups cooked **rice**

1 cup **frozen mixed vegetables**, thawed

2 tablespoons **fish sauce**

Juice of 1 **lime**

1 (15.25-ounce) can **crushed pineapple**, drained

2 **scallions**, thinly sliced

Does fried rice need shrimp and pineapple? No. But does fried rice, like, *need* shrimp and pineapple? Uh, yeah. Fish sauce gives the dish the perfect seasoning, with some sweet-salty fermented funk (though soy sauce can substitute in a pinch) while chunks of tart pineapple mingle with plump shrimp, scrambled eggs, tender vegetables, and delicious fried rice. Almost the entire food pyramid in one bowl!

1 Heat 2 tablespoons of oil in a 12-inch cast-iron skillet over medium heat. When the oil is shimmering, add the eggs. Cook, stirring often to scramble, until the eggs are just cooked through, about 2 minutes. Push the eggs to one side of the skillet and add the shrimp. Cook for 3 to 4 minutes more, until the shrimp are just opaque. Remove the eggs and shrimp to a plate.

2 Add the remaining 2 tablespoons of oil to the same skillet over medium-high heat. Add the garlic, red pepper flakes, and onion and stir until fragrant, about 1 minute. Add the rice and vegetables and stir-fry for about 5 minutes, until the rice browns slightly and the veggies are vibrant and tender. Add the eggs, shrimp, fish sauce, lime juice, and pineapple. Stir to combine and cook for 1 minute more to warm through.

3 Scoop the rice onto a serving plate and garnish with the scallions.

SERVES 4

salmon burgers
with cucumber-dill slaw

FOR THE BURGERS

1 **garlic clove**

Zest and juice of 1 **lemon**

1 large **egg**

¼ cup **fresh dill fronds**

2 tablespoons **Dijon mustard**

1 tablespoon **mayonnaise**

1 teaspoon **kosher salt**

¼ teaspoon **cayenne pepper**

1½ pounds skinless **salmon fillet**, cut into 2-inch pieces

½ cup plain **bread crumbs**

4 sesame-seed topped **hamburger buns**

3 tablespoons **olive oil**

FOR THE SLAW

¼ **cucumber**, thinly sliced

¼ medium **white onion**, thinly sliced

¼ cup **fresh dill fronds**, coarsely chopped

2 tablespoons **mayonnaise**

1 tablespoon **white wine vinegar**

Where's the beef? Who cares. These salmon burgers are delicate, delicious, and so adult, with tons of moisture. A cumber-dill slaw, dripping with savory flavor, is the only condiment you'll need. And a toasted bun pulls it all together for a burger you can't put down.

1 Make the burgers: In a food processor, combine the garlic, lemon zest and juice, egg, dill, mustard, mayonnaise, salt, and cayenne and process until smooth. Add the salmon and bread crumbs and pulse about 6 times to form a cohesive mixture with large chunks of salmon. Using your hands, shape the salmon mixture into 4 equal patties about 1 inch thick and place on a large plate. Cover with plastic and refrigerate for 30 minutes.

2 Meanwhile, make the slaw: Stir together the cucumber, onion, dill, mayonnaise, and vinegar in a small bowl. Set aside.

3 Separate the hamburger buns into halves. Heat a grill pan or large skillet over medium-high heat. Brush the grill pan with 1 tablespoon of oil and place 4 of the bun halves face down on the grill. Gently press down and grill for about 2 minutes, until nicely charred. Remove to a serving platter. Repeat with another 1 tablespoon of oil again for the remaining bun halves.

4 Brush the pan with the remaining 1 tablespoon of oil. Add the burgers to the pan and gently press down. Cook for about 5 minutes, until nicely browned, then flip. Press again and cook for about 5 minutes more, until browned on the bottom and cooked through.

5 Lay the burgers onto the buns and top with the slaw. Serve immediately.

PUT SOME
MEAT
ON YOUR BONES

PERFECT ROAST CHICKEN

SERVES 4

Every perfect adult, from Chrissy Teigen to Ina Garten, has a roast chicken recipe up their sleeve. This one is particularly easy—no twine, no basting, and no guessing how much salt is the right amount. (The answer is: a lot. But we got you.) Garlic, lemon, and thyme add just the right amount of flavor-enhancement without stealing the spotlight. And a generous rest after the oven means you have time to throw together a side like the Tomato and Haloumi Salad (see page 67). Once you make a perfect chicken, you're pretty much a perfect adult, too.

1 **lemon**, halved
1 head **garlic**
3 sprigs **fresh thyme**

4 tablespoons (½ stick) **unsalted butter**
1 (3½- to 4-pound) **whole chicken**

1 tablespoon **kosher salt**
1 teaspoon **freshly ground black pepper**

1 Set a rack in the center of the oven and preheat to 425°F.

2 Place the lemon halves face down in a 12-inch cast-iron or oven-safe skillet. Slice the top ½ inch off of the unpeeled garlic head and discard. Lay the head cut-side down in the skillet along with the thyme. Add the butter and place the skillet over high heat. Swirl occasionally to spread the butter around the skillet as it melts. Remove from the heat when the butter is melted.

3 Set the chicken on a large plate and pat dry with paper towels. Combine the salt and pepper in a small bowl. Lift the chicken vertically and use about half of the seasoning mixture, in several pinches, to season the inside cavity of the chicken. Use tongs to place the thyme, garlic, and 1 lemon half from the skillet inside the cavity. Lay the chicken back down on the plate and use tongs to squeeze the remaining lemon half over the top of the chicken.

4 Pour the melted butter from the skillet all over the chicken. Flip the chicken upside down and use about half of the remaining seasoning mixture, in several pinches, to coat the skin. Turn the chicken right-side up again and use the last of the seasoning mixture, in several pinches, to blanket the skin. Tuck the wings under the body and place the chicken into the skillet. Pour any remaining juices from the plate into the bottom of the skillet.

5 Roast for about 45 minutes, until the chicken is nicely browned all over. Remove the chicken from the oven and let it rest for about 20 minutes. An instant-read thermometer inserted into the thickest part of the thigh should read 165°F, or a small cut near the thigh should produce clear juices. Carve the chicken and serve with the pan juices.

LIFE SKILL

Here's how you carve a chicken.

1 Lay the chicken on a sturdy cutting board. Grab a big fork and a sharp knife.

2 Starting on one side, slide your knife between the drumstick and the breast, using your fork to pull the drumstick away A . Continue to cut down through the thigh until you hit the hip joint. Press hard to cut through the joint while pulling away with the fork.

3 Cut through the connective joint between the thigh and drumstick B . Lay these pieces on a serving tray.

4 Use the fork to find the spine in the center of the breast. Slide your knife just next to the spine until you hit the ribs. Use your fork to peel back the breast, and continue to run your knife just next to the ribs until you hit the wing joint C . Press hard to cut through the joint while pulling away with the fork.

5 Cut through the connective joint between the wing and breast D . Lay these pieces on the serving tray.

6 Repeat on the other side.

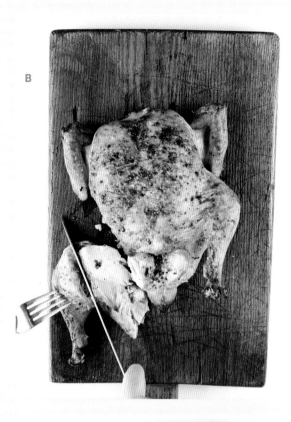

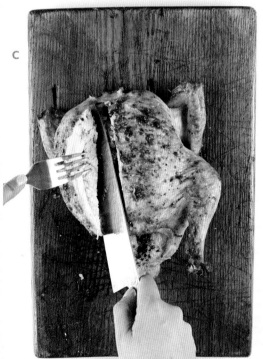

pulled pork & kimchi sliders

1 tablespoon **olive oil**

1 pound boneless **pork shoulder**, cut into 1-inch pieces

1 teaspoon **smoked paprika**

1 teaspoon **onion powder**

1 teaspoon **garlic powder**

1 tablespoon (packed) **light brown sugar**

1 tablespoon **Dijon mustard**

2 cups **lager beer**

1½ cups **kimchi**, coarsely chopped

1 (12-count) package **Hawaiian sweet rolls**

1 **Persian cucumber**, thinly sliced

If you're new to kimchi, welcome. A staple of Korean cuisine, kimchi is fermented cabbage with lots of crunch, spice, and a fermented flavor you'll be throwing on everything in no time. For those of you who've already fallen in love, be prepared to fall even harder. Here, pork shoulder is simmered with chopped kimchi and an army of flavor until it's soft and falling apart. Sweet rolls are piled with *more* kimchi, pulled pork, and an incredibly tangy sauce straight from the pan. It's the kind of crowd-pleaser you'll hate to share.

1. Heat the oil in a medium saucepan over medium-high heat. When the oil is shimmering, add the pork, paprika, onion powder, and garlic powder. Stir to coat and cook about 2 minutes, until fragrant. Add the brown sugar and mustard. Stir to coat again and cook about 2 minutes more, until the pork is slightly caramelized. Add the beer and ½ cup of the kimchi. Bring the liquid to a boil, then cover, reduce the heat to low, and cook for about 1 hour, until the meat is very tender.

2. Remove the pork from the pan and using tongs or two forks, shred it. Return the pork to the pan and increase the heat to high. Simmer, uncovered, for 10 to 15 minutes, until the liquid reduces and a thick sauce forms.

3. Take the entire block of sweet rolls and use a serrated knife to cut them through the middle, dividing them into a block of still-connected sandwich bottoms and a block of connected tops. Lay the set of bottoms on a serving platter and cover with the remaining 1 cup of kimchi. Add the pulled pork over the kimchi and spoon some of the sauce over the pork. Sprinkle the cucumber slices on top and then press the set of sandwich tops down. Have everyone reach in and pull apart a sandwich. Serve with lots of napkins!

gochujang & sesame
skirt steak

FOR THE STEAKS

1 tablespoon **rice wine vinegar**

2 tablespoons **gochujang**

1 **garlic clove**, grated or minced

¼ teaspoon **kosher salt**

½ pound **skirt steak**, cut into
   2 portions

1 tablespoon **sesame seeds**

1 tablespoon **vegetable oil**

Flaky sea salt, for topping

FOR THE SLAW

¼ cup shredded **carrots**

¼ cup **fresh cilantro leaves**,
   coarsely chopped

2 **scallions**, thinly sliced

1 tablespoon **rice wine vinegar**

Pinch of **kosher salt**

Gochujang is a Korean chile paste full of umami flavor—that super savory taste you get from soy sauce or Parmesan cheese—and just the right amount of heat. Paired with sesame and steak (more umami powerhouses!), plus a fresh, bright slaw to cut through the richness, there's a lot happening and you'll love all of it.

1 Make the steaks: Combine the vinegar, gochujang, garlic, and salt in a large ziptop bag. Add the steaks, and seal the bag tightly. Toss to coat and let marinate at room temperature for at least 1 hour or in the refrigerator for up to 24 hours. If refrigerating, rest the steaks at room temperature for 30 minutes before cooking.

2 Meanwhile, make the slaw: Combine the carrots, cilantro, scallions, vinegar, and salt in a small bowl.

3 Heat the sesame seeds in a 12-inch cast-iron skillet over high heat, stirring constantly, until fragrant and lightly toasted, about 2 minutes. Transfer to a small bowl.

4 Heat the vegetable oil in the same skillet over high heat. Remove the steaks from the bag, allowing any excess marinade to drip off. When the oil is smoking, carefully add the steaks. Cook without moving for 2 minutes, until the bottom is nicely charred. Flip and cook for 2 minutes more, until the centers are medium-rare and the outsides are charred. For a more well-done steak, cook each side 2 additional minutes.

5 Remove the steaks to a cutting board and loosely cover with foil. Let them rest for 5 minutes. Slice each steak against the grain in thin pieces. Lay each steak on a serving plate and season with flaky salt. Spoon the slaw evenly on top of the steaks and sprinkle the sesame seeds over everything before serving.

cozy chicken & dumplings

FOR THE SOUP

2 tablespoons **vegetable oil**

2 pounds boneless, skinless **chicken breasts**, cut into 1-inch pieces

Kosher salt and **freshly ground black pepper**

1 cup diced **yellow onion**

2 medium **carrots**, sliced

3 **garlic cloves**, minced

5 tablespoons **unsalted butter**

6 tablespoons **all-purpose flour**

6 cups **chicken broth** (see page 46) or store-bought **chicken stock**

½ cup **heavy cream**

1 sprig **fresh thyme**

2 **dried bay leaves**

1½ cups **frozen peas**

FOR THE DUMPLINGS

2 cups **all-purpose flour**

1 tablespoon **baking powder**

½ teaspoon **kosher salt**

½ teaspoon **freshly ground black pepper**

1⅓ cups **heavy cream**

¼ cup **fresh parsley leaves**, minced

LIFE SKILL

Flour + butter + heat = roux. Roux acts as a thickener once liquid joins the pot. The most important part is cooking the flour just long enough to take on a golden color and nutty smell.

Chicken pot pie is great. No one is saying it's not. But chicken and dumplings provide more of what you actually want—saucy dough! A delicious, thick chicken base gets covered in very simply made dumplings. A few minutes of simmering later and you'll lift the lid to find—like magic!—giant, fluffy clouds of dough just begging to be dunked in chicken gravy. We recommend you break out your coziest sweater for this cozy dish!

1 Make the soup: Heat the oil in a Dutch oven over medium-high heat. When the oil is shimmering, add the chicken and season with salt and pepper. Cook, stirring occasionally, until browned on the outside and cooked through, about 6 minutes. Remove to a plate and set aside.

2 Add the onion and carrots to the pot and season with salt and pepper. Cook until the onion is softened and the carrots are tender, about 3 minutes. Add the garlic and cook for about 1 minute more, until fragrant.

3 Reduce the heat to medium-low and add the butter and flour and cook, stirring constantly to prevent lumps from forming, for 3 minutes, until the flour is lightly golden. Return the chicken and any accumulated juices back to the pot and stir to coat in the roux. Add the chicken broth and stir to dissolve the flour mixture. Add the cream, thyme, and bay leaves and bring to a simmer. Add the frozen peas, cover, and simmer for 15 minutes, until the soup is thick and creamy.

4 Meanwhile, make the dumplings: Stir together the flour, baking powder, salt, pepper, and cream in a large bowl until a ball of cohesive dough forms. Use a soup spoon or a small cookie scoop to form about a dozen 1-inch dough balls on a plate.

5 Remove the lid from the pot and remove the thyme sprig and bay leaves. Taste for seasoning. Place the balls into the soup. Add the parsley and cover. Simmer for about 15 minutes more, until the dumplings are cooked through. Fill bowls with a large ladle of soup and 2 dumplings.

General Tso's chicken wings
with fried broccoli

FOR THE WINGS

2 pounds **chicken wings**

¼ cup plus 1 teaspoon **cornstarch**

1 teaspoon **kosher salt**

¼ cup **soy sauce**

3 tablespoons **honey**

2 tablespoons **ketchup**

2 **garlic cloves**, grated or minced

2 teaspoons minced **fresh ginger**

1 teaspoon **rice vinegar**

1 teaspoon **toasted sesame oil**

1 teaspoon **red pepper flakes**

8 cups **vegetable oil**

FOR THE BROCCOLI

¼ cup **cornstarch**

¼ cup **all-purpose flour**

1 teaspoon **baking powder**

1 teaspoon **kosher salt**

1 (1-pound) head **broccoli**, cut into large chicken wing–size florets

LIFE SKILL

Letting the chicken wings come to room temperature before frying ensures an even cooking time when they hit the oil. The salt and cornstarch will dry out the chicken skin and give an extra-crispy coating.

Skip the delivery app and try this recipe. Gooey, sweet, and spicy, these crispy fried chicken wings are blanketed in a delicious General Tso's sauce. Broccoli gets lightly coated in batter and quick-fried for a salty crunch that almost—almost!—steals the spotlight. Get ready for a serious case of the munchies!

1 Set a rack in the center of the oven and preheat to 250°F. Line a rimmed baking sheet with foil and set a wire rack on top.

2 Pat the wings dry with paper towels. In a large bowl, toss the chicken wings with ¼ cup of the cornstarch and the salt. Set the wings on the wire rack to dry out for at least 20 minutes or up to 1 hour.

3 Meanwhile, make the sauce. Whisk together the soy sauce, honey, ketchup, garlic, ginger, rice vinegar, sesame oil, red pepper flakes, and remaining 1 teaspoon of cornstarch in a large bowl until well combined.

4 Heat the oil in a Dutch oven over medium-high heat. Use an instant-read thermometer to check periodically until the oil hits 375°F. Working in batches, use tongs to carefully lower about one-third of the wings into the oil. Fry them for about 12 minutes, until the coating is nicely browned and very crisp. Use tongs to transfer the finished wings back to the wire rack. Allow the oil to return to 375°F between batches.

5 When all the wings have been fried, use tongs to transfer them to the sauce. Toss to coat thoroughly, then transfer back to the wire rack. Bake in the oven for about 10 minutes until the sauce is sticky and sizzling.

6 Meanwhile, make the broccoli: In a separate medium bowl, whisk together the cornstarch, flour, baking powder, salt, and ½ cup of water to make a smooth paste. Add the broccoli and toss to coat in a thin layer of batter. Allow the oil to return to 375°F and use tongs to fry the broccoli in two batches for about 5 minutes each, until the broccoli is crisp. Transfer to paper towels as each batch is finished.

7 Remove the wings from the oven. Pile a serving tray with wings and broccoli and serve immediately.

cheesesteak
quesadilla

1 tablespoon **olive oil**

½ pound **skirt steak**

Kosher salt and **freshly ground black pepper**

1 medium **white onion**, halved and sliced

1 **green bell pepper**, cut into large strips

2 large **flour tortillas**

8 slices **provolone cheese**

Chopped fresh parsley and **salsa con queso**, for serving

If you've ever wished you could pick up all the melty goodness of a Philly cheesesteak and then aim it towards a bowl of more cheese, a) you're a hero and b) welcome home. Skirt steak is not the most luxurious cut of meat, so letting it rest and slicing it thinly are always two crucial steps. Thick-cut vegetables, cooked to just-tender, will give you much-needed crunch in every bite. It's pure cheesy pleasure from there on out.

1 Heat the oil in a medium skillet over medium-high heat. Season the steak on both sides with salt and black pepper. When the oil is shimmering, add the steak and cook for 2 minutes, until the bottom is charred. Flip and cook for another 2 to 3 minutes, until medium-rare. (Cook 2 to 3 minutes more, flipping halfway, for well-done.) Remove the steak to a cutting board and loosely cover with foil to rest.

2 Meanwhile, add the onion and bell pepper to the skillet and cook for about 5 minutes, until crisp-tender. Remove to a plate. Slice the steak against the grain into thin strips.

3 In the same skillet, place a tortilla and add 2 slices of cheese. Layer on half of the steak and vegetables and 2 more slices of cheese on top. Fold the tortilla in half over itself and cook for 3 minutes, until the bottom is nicely toasted. Flip and cook for 3 minutes more, until the cheese is melted. Repeat with the remaining tortilla, cheese, steak, and vegetables.

4 Cut each quesadilla into 4 pieces. Serve with parsley sprinkled on top and queso alongside.

down south jambalaya

2 tablespoons **olive oil**

1 pound boneless, skinless **chicken thighs**, cut into 1-inch pieces

1 tablespoon **Cajun seasoning**

2 teaspoons **kosher salt**

1 teaspoon **freshly ground black pepper**

1 teaspoon **garlic powder**

1 teaspoon **smoked paprika**

1 teaspoon **cayenne pepper**

4 cooked **andouille sausages**, sliced into ½-inch-thick rounds

1 medium **yellow onion**, diced

2 stalks **celery**, diced

1 **green bell pepper**, diced

1 **jalapeño**, minced

6 **garlic cloves**, minced

1½ cups **chicken broth** (see page 46) or store-bought **chicken stock**

1 (14.5-ounce) can **crushed tomatoes**

1 pound **jumbo shrimp**, peeled, deveined, and tails removed

2 cups cooked **rice**

The signature dish of Louisiana is a densely spiced rice dish influenced by the West African, Spanish, and French melting pot of the state. A trio of meats—chicken, sausage, and shrimp—might not seem like ideal partners, but the combination, heavily seasoned of course, elevates the bowl to extreme heights of Creole goodness.

1 Heat 1 tablespoon of the oil in a Dutch oven over medium-high heat. When the oil is shimmering, add the chicken, Cajun seasoning, 1 teaspoon of salt, the black pepper, garlic powder, paprika, and cayenne. Stir to coat the chicken with the spices then cook for about 5 minutes, until the meat is cooked through. Add the sausages and cook for about 3 minutes more, until warmed through. Remove the meat to a large plate.

2 Add the remaining 1 tablespoon of oil to the Dutch oven. When the oil shimmers, add the onion, celery, bell pepper, jalapeño, garlic, and remaining 1 teaspoon of salt. Cook until the vegetables have softened and started to brown, 8 to 10 minutes.

3 Add the chicken broth and tomatoes to the pot. Return the chicken and sausages to the pot along with any collected juices. Bring the liquid to a simmer, then cover and simmer for about 10 minutes, until the broth is bubbling and the flavors have fully incorporated. Stir in the shrimp, cover, and simmer for about 5 minutes more, until the shrimp is just opaque. Divide the rice among four bowls and top with a big scoop of jambalaya.

pork & mushroom ragu
with polenta

FOR THE PORK

1 medium **carrot**, cut into thirds

1 medium **fennel bulb**,
  cut into quarters

1 medium **white onion**,
  cut into quarters

1 **garlic clove**

½ teaspoon **kosher salt**

1 sprig **fresh rosemary**,
  stem removed

1 sprig **fresh thyme**,
  stem removed

1 sprig **fresh sage**,
  stem removed

2 tablespoons **olive oil**

1 cup **chicken broth**
  (see page 46) or store-bought
  chicken stock

2 tablespoons **fresh lemon juice**

1 pound **ground pork**

2 **portobello mushrooms**,
  stemmed and cut into ½-inch
  pieces

4 **shiitake mushrooms**, stemmed
  and cut into ½-inch pieces

1 (14.5-ounce) can **diced
  tomatoes**

FOR THE POLENTA

1 cup **coarse-ground polenta**

½ teaspoon **kosher salt**

4 tablespoons (½ stick)
  unsalted butter

2 tablespoons grated
  Parmesan cheese

Chopped **fresh parsley**,
  for serving

A creamy bowl of polenta—the Italian equivalent of grits—basically begs for a swirl of something savory. Pork ragu gets an extra boost of savory with two types of mushrooms—and if the word *ragu* conjures images of having to guard a pot all day, forget it. This shortcut recipe maintains all the depth of flavor with barely any of the time commitment. Made in a big batch, you'll have plenty to carry you through the week.

1 Make the pork: In a food processor, combine the carrot, fennel, onion, garlic, ¼ teaspoon of salt, and the rosemary, thyme, and sage leaves and pulse for about 1 minute, until finely chopped. Scrape down the sides as needed.

2 Heat the oil in a large skillet over medium heat. When the oil is shimmering, add the vegetable mixture. Cook, stirring occasionally, until the liquid evaporates and the vegetables begin to brown, 13 to 15 minutes. Add the chicken broth and lemon juice. Use a wooden spoon to scrape up any browned bits from the bottom of the pan. Cook until the liquid mostly evaporates, about 5 minutes.

3 Add the pork, mushrooms, and the remaining ¼ teaspoon of salt. Cook, breaking up the pork with a wooden spoon, until mostly browned, about 4 minutes. Add the tomatoes and simmer for about 30 minutes, until the sauce is thick.

4 Meanwhile, make the polenta: Bring 3 cups of water to a boil in a medium saucepan over medium-high heat. Slowly whisk in the polenta. Bring the polenta to a boil, then reduce the heat to medium-low. Continue whisking the polenta periodically for about 20 minutes, until it's creamy but still slightly firm. Then add the salt, butter, and Parmesan and whisk to combine.

5 Divide the polenta among eight bowls and spoon the ragu over the top. Garnish with parsley and serve.

better-than-mom's
meat loaf

2 large **egg yolks**

¾ cup plain **bread crumbs**

½ cup grated **Parmesan cheese**

¼ cup **sour cream** or plain
  Greek yogurt

¼ cup **chicken broth**
  (see page 46) or store-bought
  chicken stock

2 tablespoons **ketchup**

1 tablespoon **kosher salt**

1 tablespoon **onion powder**

1 tablespoon **dried parsley**

1 teaspoon **garlic powder**

1 teaspoon **chili powder**

1 teaspoon **dried oregano**

1 teaspoon **smoked paprika**

1 teaspoon **ground cumin**

1 teaspoon **freshly ground
  black pepper**

2 pounds **ground beef**, 80% lean

FOR THE GLAZE

½ cup **ketchup**

¼ cup **red wine vinegar**

3 tablespoons (packed)
  light brown sugar

1 teaspoon **hot sauce**

½ teaspoon **ground cumin**

LIFE SKILL

Fear not! Resting meat
doesn't mean cold food.
You're just giving it time
to redistribute juices and
relax the fibers. Translation?
Tender, juicy, and still warm.

Listen, nothing can actually compete with Mom's recipe because
the most special ingredient of all—love—is unquantifiable and rare.

Did your mom stop reading over your shoulder? Ok, cool, let's
talk over here. Meat loaf is almost always dry, but it doesn't have
to be! This recipe uses only egg yolks, as we have found that the
whites are useless and the main culprit for dryness—plus sour
cream and broth add a ton of moisture. Layers and layers of flavor
in the loaf and in the glaze keep the beef from tasting overwhelm-
ingly, well, beefy. And coming in at medium-rare and letting the
cooking finish during a long rest time means you'll have cooked-
through meat without cooked-to-death texture. Love ya, Mom.

1 Set a rack in the center of the oven and preheat to 400°F. Line a
   rimmed baking sheet with parchment paper.

2 Make the meat loaf: Whisk together the egg yolks, bread crumbs,
   Parmesan, sour cream, chicken broth, ketchup, salt, onion powder,
   parsley, garlic powder, chili powder, oregano, paprika, cumin, and
   black pepper in a large bowl. Add the beef and use clean hands to
   fully incorporate the seasonings; be careful not to overmix. Transfer
   the mixture to the baking sheet and shape into an approximately
   10 by 5-inch rectangle. Bake for about 60 minutes, until the meat is
   browned and an instant-read thermometer inserted into the center
   reads between 145°F and 150°F.

3 Meanwhile, make the glaze: Whisk together the ketchup, red wine
   vinegar, brown sugar, hot sauce, and cumin in a small saucepan over
   medium-high heat. Simmer, whisking occasionally, until reduced and
   thickened, about 15 minutes.

4 Remove the meat loaf from the oven and cover with the glaze,
   brushing all sides. Return the meat loaf to the oven and bake for
   about 5 minutes more, until the glaze is bubbling and caramelized.
   Loosely cover with foil and let the meat loaf rest for about 20 minutes
   before serving.

RABBIT
FOOD

CHEESE-STUFFED VEGGIE BURGER DELUXE

SERVES 4

Let's face it, frozen veggie burgers can be a real veggie bummer. They seem to fall into two camps: packed with processed soy and binders, or loaded with freeze-dried vegetables that crumble. Never again. Here's a veggie burger with a variety of clean protein sources and tons of fiber, plus great flavor and a texture that holds up on the grill. And because adulting doesn't have to be serious all the time, we've stuffed the burgers with a pool of delicious melty cheese. Whether you're vegan, veg-, pesc-, flex-, or just taking a breather from red meat, here's a burger for the people.

1 (15.5-ounce) can **kidney beans**, drained and rinsed

½ cup **raw cashews**

¼ cup **old-fashioned rolled oats**

¼ cup cooked **quinoa**

¼ cup grated **Parmesan cheese** or ¼ cup **nutritional yeast**

1 teaspoon **chili powder**

½ teaspoon **ground cumin**

½ teaspoon **smoked paprika**

½ teaspoon **kosher salt**

½ teaspoon **freshly ground black pepper**

2 large **egg yolks** or 1 tablespoon **ground chia** or **ground flaxseed** soaked in 3 tablespoons water

½ medium **red onion**, coarsely chopped

4 slices **American cheese** or **vegan cheese slices** (optional)

¼ cup shredded **mozzarella cheese** or **vegan shredded cheese** (optional)

4 sesame-seed topped **hamburger buns**

3 tablespoons **olive oil**

Sliced **beefsteak tomatoes**, thinly sliced **red onion**, **lettuce**, **ketchup**, **mustard**, and **mayonnaise**, for topping (optional)

1. Set a rack in the center of the oven and preheat the oven to 375°F.

2. Spread the kidney beans on one side and the cashews on the opposite side of a rimmed baking sheet **A**. Bake for about 10 minutes, until the cashews are golden brown and the kidney beans have split and dried. Let cool for 10 minutes.

3. In a food processor, combine the toasted cashews, oats, quinoa, Parmesan, chili powder, cumin, paprika, salt, and pepper. Pulse about 20 times, until a sandy mixture forms. Add the eggs, onion, and beans. Pulse about 10 more times to form a thick, wet mixture **B**. Divide the burger mixture into 4 even portions.

4. If stuffing the burgers with cheese, lay out the slices of American cheese and place 1 tablespoon of mozzarella in the center of each. Fold and squeeze the American cheese into a tight ball around the mozzarella **C**. Press the cheese ball into the center of each burger and fold the mixture around it **D**.

5. Press the burgers into a wide, flat patty, about ½ inch thick.

6. Separate the hamburger buns into halves. Heat a grill pan or large skillet over medium-high heat. Brush the grill pan with 1 tablespoon of oil and place 4 of the bun halves in the pan **E**. Gently press down and grill for about 2 minutes, until nicely charred. Remove to a serving platter. Repeat with another 1 tablespoon of oil for the remaining bun halves. Remove to the serving platter.

7. Brush the pan with the remaining 1 tablespoon of oil. Add the 4 burgers to the pan and gently press down. Cook for about 5 minutes, until nicely charred, then flip **F**. Press again and cook for about 5 minutes more, until the bottoms have charred and the cheese in the middle has melted.

8. Assemble the burgers with any combination of tomatoes, onion, lettuce, ketchup, mustard, and mayo. (We say load them all on!)

roasted eggplant curry

2 medium **globe eggplants**

½ cup **vegetable oil**

Kosher salt and **freshly ground black pepper**

½ medium **white onion**, finely chopped

2½ tablespoons **curry powder**

3 **garlic cloves**, minced

1 (1-inch) piece **fresh ginger**, peeled and minced

3 **Roma tomatoes**, diced

1 (13.5-ounce) can full-fat **coconut milk**

Cooked **rice**, for serving

Chopped **fresh cilantro**, for serving

Eggplant is an uncelebrated vegetable that deserves more love. A powerhouse of vitamins and minerals, eggplant isn't a wimpy wilter like spinach. It's dense enough to take on aggressive cooking and still come out standing. Friendly to almost all dietary restrictions, this eggplant curry is an ingenious way to fill a bowl with plant-based goodness that will keep you full and nourished.

1 Set a rack in the center of the oven and preheat to 400°F.

2 Cut the tops off the eggplants and discard. Cube the eggplants and spread them on a rimmed baking sheet. Toss with ¼ cup of the vegetable oil and season with salt and pepper. Bake for about 25 minutes, tossing halfway through, until soft and golden brown.

3 Heat the remaining ¼ cup of vegetable oil in a Dutch oven over medium-low heat. When the oil is shimmering, add the onion and cook, stirring occasionally, until the onion is softened and beginning to brown, about 8 minutes. Stir in the curry powder, garlic, and ginger, and season generously with salt and pepper. Cook for about 1 minute more, until fragrant.

4 Add the tomatoes, coconut milk, and ½ cup of water. Stir to combine. Add the roasted eggplants and stir once more. Bring the curry to a simmer, then cover and reduce the heat to low. Cook for about 25 minutes, until the sauce has reduced and slightly thickened.

5 Serve the curry over rice and top with cilantro.

A

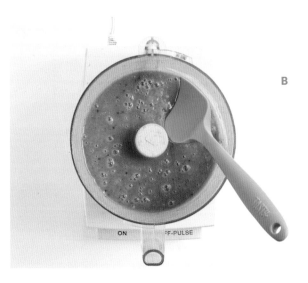

B

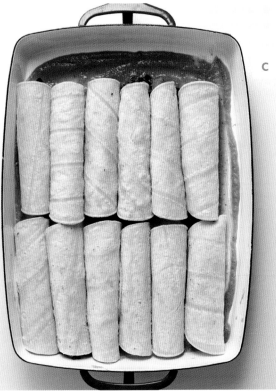

C

pumpkin enchiladas

FOR THE ENCHILADAS

1 pound peeled and cubed **butternut squash**

1 tablespoon **olive oil**

Kosher salt and **freshly ground black pepper**

3 cups chopped **kale**

1 (15.5-ounce) can **black beans**, drained and rinsed

1 **garlic clove**, minced

½ teaspoon **smoked paprika**

½ teaspoon **ground cumin**

½ teaspoon **chili powder**

12 (6-inch) **corn tortillas**

1 cup crumbled **Cotija cheese**

FOR THE PUMPKIN SAUCE

1 (15-ounce) can **pumpkin puree**

1 **jalapeño**, stem removed

5 **garlic cloves**

1 teaspoon **chili powder**

½ teaspoon **kosher salt**

Yes, these enchiladas are technically filled with squash, kale, and black beans—a picture of nutrients, fiber, and protein. But the thing you'll remember most about this dish is the incredibly simple and highly effective pumpkin sauce. The enchilada fillings can rotate with whatever you need to use up—a tortilla is always a great vessel for leftovers!—but keep that can of pumpkin in your pantry at all times and slather it on whenever you need a delicious life hack.

1. Set a rack in the center of the oven and preheat to 400°F.

2. Make the enchiladas: Toss the squash and oil on a rimmed baking sheet. Season with salt and pepper. Roast for about 30 minutes, stirring halfway through, until tender and starting to brown. Remove the squash from the oven and add the kale, black beans, garlic, paprika, cumin, and chili powder to the hot baking sheet. Stir together to wilt the kale and toast the spices A .

3. Meanwhile, make the pumpkin sauce: In a blender or food processor, combine the pumpkin, jalapeño, garlic, chili powder, salt, and ½ cup of water. Blend until smooth, scraping down the sides as needed, about 2 minutes B .

4. Stack the tortillas, wrap them in foil, and place the packet directly on the oven rack. Heat for about 5 minutes, until slightly softened and warmed through. Unwrap the packet, being careful of the hot steam collected inside.

5. Spread half of the pumpkin sauce across the bottom of a 9 by 13-inch baking pan. Separate the squash mixture into 12 equal portions on the sheet pan. Fill a tortilla with 1 portion of vegetables and roll it up. Place the tortilla seam-side down in the pan. Repeat with the remaining tortillas, tucking them snuggly in two equal rows C . Top with the remaining pumpkin sauce and the Cotija.

6. Bake for about 20 minutes, until the cheese begins to brown. Let cool for about 10 minutes before serving.

stewed beans
with parmesan bread crumbs

FOR THE BEANS

1 (14.5-ounce) can **crushed tomatoes**

2 sprigs **fresh thyme**

2 **dried bay leaves**

1 **garlic clove**, smashed

1 (1 pound 13-ounce) can **butter beans**, drained and rinsed

Kosher salt and **freshly ground black pepper**

FOR THE BREAD CRUMBS

1 tablespoon **olive oil**

¼ cup plain **bread crumbs**

¼ teaspoon **garlic powder**

½ tablespoon grated **Parmesan cheese**

½ teaspoon **dried oregano**

1 teaspoon finely chopped **fresh parsley**

Sometimes the simplest dishes can be the most comforting. This dish is greater than the sum of its parts, with classic flavors of tomato, thyme, and garlic, mixed with butter beans, under a dusting of bread crumbs, somehow adding up to the kind of meal you'll feel like you've been making forever. And even if you haven't been, we hope it becomes a new back-pocket classic for you.

1 Make the beans: Combine the tomatoes, thyme, bay leaves, and garlic in a medium saucepan over medium heat. Simmer the sauce, stirring occasionally, until it's thick and slightly reduced, about 15 minutes. Stir in the beans and season with salt and pepper. Cover and reduce the heat to low while making the bread crumbs.

2 Make the bread crumbs: Add the olive oil, bread crumbs, garlic powder, Parmesan, oregano, and parsley to a medium skillet over medium heat. Stir well to coat and toast for about 5 minutes, continuing to stir occasionally, until the bread crumbs are nicely browned and the seasonings are fragrant.

3 Transfer the stewed beans to a serving bowl. Remove and discard the thyme sprig and bay leaves. Sprinkle half of the bread crumbs over the top. Serve the stewed beans with the remaining bread crumbs alongside.

stuffed peppers
with spiced quinoa & feta

4 medium **bell peppers**

1¼ teaspoons **kosher salt**

3 tablespoons **olive oil**

1 medium **shallot**, minced

2 **garlic cloves**, minced

½ teaspoon **ground cumin**

½ teaspoon **ground turmeric**

½ teaspoon **smoked paprika**

½ teaspoon **ground cinnamon**

¼ teaspoon **freshly ground black pepper**

1 cup dry **quinoa**, rinsed and drained

1¾ cups **vegetable broth**

¼ cup **sliced almonds**

¼ cup **toasted pecans**, coarsely chopped

¼ cup **golden raisins**

¼ cup **dried cranberries**

¼ cup crumbled **feta cheese**

Some vegetarian dishes try to make up for the lack of meat, while some improve on the omission and make the dish even greater. A heavily spiced stuffing packed with quinoa, fruit, nuts, and feta mingles so well with the warm pepper and creates a dish that feels brand new and deeply nostalgic at the same time. To really take advantage of your day, make the stuffing in the morning and fill the peppers that night for dinner.

1 Set a rack in the center of the oven and preheat to 400°F.

2 Slice the tops off of the bell peppers and scoop out the seeds and white ribs. Place the peppers in an 8 by 8-inch baking pan or a 9-inch deep-dish pie pan. Season the insides of the peppers with ½ teaspoon of salt.

3 Heat the oil in a large saucepan over medium-high heat. When the oil is shimmering, add the shallot and cook for about 5 minutes, until softened. Add the garlic, cumin, turmeric, paprika, cinnamon, and black pepper. Cook for 1 minute more, until the spices are fragrant.

4 Add the quinoa and toast slightly, about 2 minutes. Add the vegetable broth and ½ teaspoon of salt. Bring the liquid to a boil and then cover the pan and reduce the heat to low. Cook for 15 minutes, then remove the pot from the heat, keeping the lid on. Let steam for about 5 minutes before removing the lid and fluffing the quinoa. Stir in the almonds, pecans, raisins, cranberries, and feta.

5 Fill each pepper to the top with the quinoa stuffing. (Reserve any extra stuffing for delicious leftovers!) Pour ¾ cup of water into the bottom of the pan along with the remaining ¼ teaspoon of salt. Tightly cover the pan in foil and transfer to the oven. Bake for 40 to 45 minutes, until the water has evaporated and the peppers are tender.

broc tocs

½ medium **shallot**, thinly sliced

Juice of 1 **lime**

Kosher salt

1 head **broccoli**, cut into small florets

1 tablespoon **olive oil**

6 (6-inch) **flour tortillas**

1 cup shredded **Mexican blend cheese**

6 **hard taco shells**

Crumbled **feta cheese** and **hot sauce**, for serving

Broccoli in tacos? Don't broc it till you've tried it. A smoky char in the oven and a firm bite make this cruciferous veg a surprisingly great filling. A little pickled shallot adds a punch of acidity, and feta brings an unexpected salty richness. And a tortilla melted around a taco shell? C'mon!

1 Set racks in the center and lower third of the oven and preheat the oven to 450°F.

2 Toss the shallot and lime juice with a generous pinch of salt in a small bowl. Set aside.

3 Toss the broccoli and oil with a generous pinch of salt on a rimmed baking sheet. Bake on the center rack for 20 minutes, tossing halfway through, until the broccoli is tender and charred in places.

4 Arrange the tortillas on a separate rimmed baking sheet. Evenly divide the cheese among the tortillas, being sure it reaches to the edges. Bake on the lower rack for 5 minutes, until the cheese is melted. Remove the baking sheet from the oven and lay 1 taco shell on its side onto 1 tortilla, gently pressing it into the cheese. Use a spatula to fold the other end of the tortilla around the shell and press again, careful not to break the shell. Repeat with the remaining shells and tortillas. Cool slightly on the baking sheet.

5 Divide the broccoli mixture equally among the taco shells. Add some pickled shallot. Sprinkle feta over the top and finish with hot sauce.

creamy mushroom
toasts

2 tablespoons **olive oil**

3 **garlic cloves**, minced

1 teaspoon **smoked paprika**, plus more for serving

14 ounces sliced mixed **mushrooms**

1 teaspoon **kosher salt**

¼ cup **heavy cream**

3 **scallions**, thinly sliced

4 large **eggs**

4 (1-inch-thick) slices crusty **sourdough** or **multigrain bread**

Once in a while, you find the rare dish that seems like it could be breakfast, brunch, lunch, or dinner. Sure, there are I'm-too-lazy things—cereal and oatmeal are fantastic anytime. But a real cross-over hit is hard to come by. A mix of savory mushrooms tossed in cream gets piled on thick-cut toast and topped with a poached egg. Does that not sound like exactly what you want *right now*?

1 Bring a medium saucepan of water to a boil over medium heat.

2 Meanwhile, heat 1 tablespoon of oil in a large skillet over medium heat. When the oil is shimmering, add the garlic and cook for about 1 minute, until fragrant. Add the paprika, mushrooms, and salt. Cook, stirring occasionally, for about 10 minutes, until the mushrooms are nicely browned. Add the heavy cream and three-quarters of the scallions. Stir to combine, then transfer the mushrooms to a bowl. Wipe out the skillet.

3 Working one at a time, crack an egg into a small bowl. Lower the rim of the bowl into the saucepan of boiling water and gently tip the egg in. Repeat with the remaining 3 eggs. Cook the eggs for 2 to 4 minutes, until the whites are set but the yolks are still soft. Remove the eggs to a paper towel to drain.

4 In the skillet from the mushrooms, heat the remaining 1 tablespoon of oil over high heat. When the oil is shimmering, add the slices of bread and gently press down. Toast for about 2 minutes, until golden brown, then flip and toast for about 2 minutes more.

5 Place 2 pieces of toast on two plates. Divide the mushroom mixture among the toast slices and lay a poached egg on top of the mushrooms. Sprinkle each with a pinch of paprika and garnish with the reserved scallions.

LIFE SKILL

Forget what you've heard about swirling water or adding vinegar to poach eggs. The easiest way is to get the water boiling and slide the egg right in. Cracking into a bowl first allows you to catch any shell (see page 156), and to lower the rim right to the surface of the water for the most delicate slide ever.

vegetarian "lobster" rolls

2 (14-ounce) cans **hearts of palm**, drained

1 large stalk **celery**, diced

2 tablespoons chopped **fresh dill**

3 tablespoons chopped **fresh chives**

2 teaspoons **Old Bay seasoning**

⅓ cup **mayonnaise**

2 **lemons**

8 New England–style top-split **hot dog buns** or 4 standard **hot dog buns**

2 tablespoons **unsalted butter**, melted

If you've ever stared at a heart of palm and wondered what on earth you could do with it, here is your answer. For those who can't stomach lobster—or even those who can't stomach the cost of lobster—these dressed-up hearts of palm still give the feeling of instant summer. A couple teaspoons of Old Bay bring the spray of the ocean and the cry of the gulls into a simply prepared salad that's piled into butter-soaked toasted buns. You'll feel like your toes are dangling right off the pier.

1 Cut the hearts of palm into uneven 1- to 2-inch diagonal pieces and add them to a large bowl. Add the celery, dill, 2 tablespoons of chives, the Old Bay, and mayonnaise and stir to combine. Add the juice of 1 lemon. Stir to mix again.

2 Heat a medium skillet over medium heat. If using top-split hot dog buns, brush the outsides with the butter and place in the skillet to toast on each side for about 2 minutes, until golden. If using standard buns, brush the insides with butter and press the butter side down onto the skillet to toast for about 2 minutes, until golden.

3 Cut the remaining lemon into 8 wedges. Fill the buns with the hearts of palm mixture and garnish with the remaining 1 tablespoon of chives. Serve with the lemon wedges for squeezing.

LIFE SKILL

No one wants lemon seeds in their food. Hold a cupped hand and squeeze the lemon directly into it. Let the juice trickle through your fingers, then toss out the seeds. This trick works for any citrus.

A SWEET FINISH

CONFETTI CAKE CHEESECAKE

SERVES 8 TO 10

A confetti cake is childish. Cheesecake is peak Golden Girls. So the average of this particular recipe lands somewhere that's safely adult. (Don't check the calculation—just go with it.) And "why have one when you can have two" is math we can all agree on when it comes to dessert. Fluffy box cake, one of life's great pleasures, acts as the crust for a perfectly tart cheesecake. Some whipped cream from the can and sprinkles proudly declare that age is only a number. Whether you're celebrating a twenty-mumble or fifth-annual thirty-first birthday, this cake is here for the celebration.

Nonstick cooking spray

1 box **confetti cake mix**, plus additional ingredients according to box instructions

1 cup **milk**

1 tablespoon **unflavored gelatin**

32 ounces **cream cheese**, at room temperature

1 cup **sugar**

1 tablespoon **vanilla extract**

Whipped cream, for serving

Rainbow sprinkles, for serving

1   Set a rack in the center of the oven and preheat to 350°F. Lightly coat a 10- or 11-inch springform pan with nonstick spray.

2   Prepare the cake mix according to the box directions and pour the batter into the prepared springform pan. Bake for about 35 minutes, or according to the box directions, until a toothpick comes out dry when inserted into the center. Let cool completely in the pan, about 2 hours.

3   In a large microwave-safe bowl, microwave the milk on high for 90 seconds until it's hot, then whisk in the gelatin until dissolved. Add the cream cheese, sugar, and vanilla and whisk until fully combined. Pour the cheesecake mixture over the cooled cake. Loosely cover with plastic wrap and chill in the refrigerator for at least 3 hours or up to 12 hours.

4   Run a butter knife around the edge of the springform pan and carefully remove the outer ring. Decorate the cake with whipped cream and sprinkles before serving.

flourless chocolate
dream cake

Nonstick cooking spray

3 (3-ounce) bars **bittersweet chocolate**

1 stick **unsalted butter**, cubed

1 teaspoon **orange zest**

1 tablespoon **fresh orange juice**

6 large **eggs**

1 cup **granulated sugar**

2 cups cold **heavy cream**

¼ cup **powdered sugar**

1 teaspoon **vanilla extract**

2 tablespoons **unsweetened cocoa powder**

Can something be way too much and not quite enough at the same time? Have you ever watched someone's mouth say, "I'm so full" while their eyes flicker with the fantasy of one more slice? Have you said, "Get this away from me" and then clutched the plate with rigor mortis? Dense on the inside, meringue-like on the outside, a dramatic amount of whipped cream on top . . . was this cake all a dream? Or will the leftovers be waiting for you to take another bite at midnight?

1 Set a rack in the center of the oven and preheat to 350°F. Lightly coat an 8- or 9-inch springform pan with nonstick spray and set it on a rimmed baking sheet.

2 Chop one of the chocolate bars into equal thirds. Set one of the thirds aside. Finely chop the remaining 2⅔ bars of chocolate. Add the chopped chocolate and butter to a medium microwave-safe bowl. Microwave on high for 90 seconds, using a spatula to stir every 30 seconds A , until the chocolate is completely melted. (Continue to microwave in 15-second intervals if the chocolate hasn't melted.) Stir in the orange zest and juice.

3 Separate the egg yolks and whites into two separate large bowls (see note, page 156). Use an electric mixer on low to whip the whites until they're foamy and just starting to hold shape, 2 to 3 minutes B , then add ½ cup granulated sugar and continue whisking on medium-high for 1 to 2 minutes more until the whites are glossy and soft peaks form.

(recipe continues)

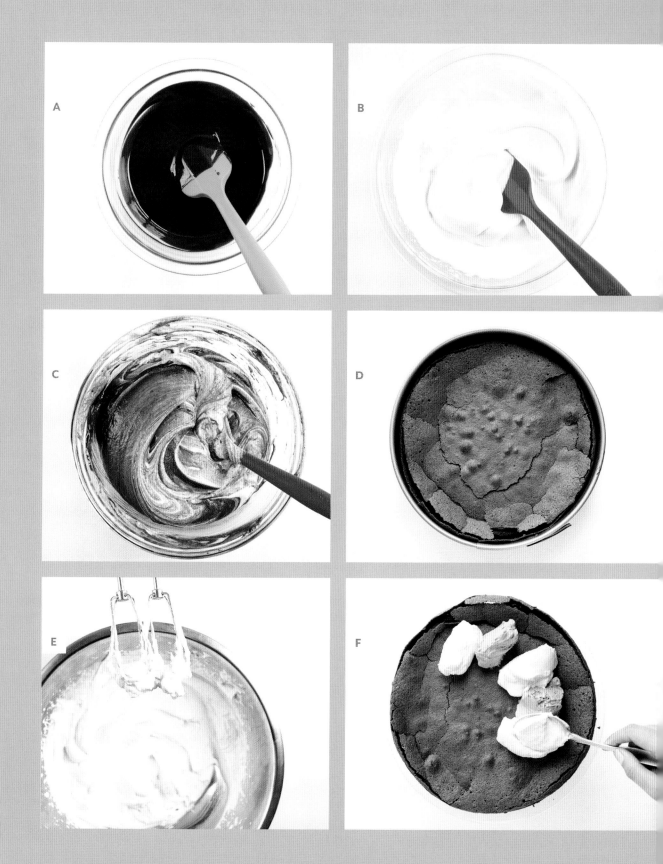

4   Use the electric mixer on low to whisk the egg yolks with the remaining ½ cup of granulated sugar until the yolks are smooth and thick, about 1 minute. Add the chocolate mixture to the yolks and continue whisking on low to combine, about 1 more minute. Use a spatula to scoop one-third of the egg whites into the chocolate mixture and gently fold to incorporate C . Add the remainder of the egg whites and fold again until just mixed. Be careful not to deflate or overmix the batter.

5   Pour the batter into the prepared springform pan and transfer, along with the baking sheet, to the oven. Bake for about 35 minutes, until the cake is puffed and no longer jiggly. Let cool completely in the springform pan set on a trivet or wire rack, 1 to 2 hours. The cake will rise in the oven and then crack and form a pit in the center as it cools D .

6   To serve, run a knife around the edge of the springform and carefully remove the outer ring. In a large bowl, use an electric mixer, starting on low and gradually increasing to medium-high, to whip the heavy cream until soft peaks form, 3 to 4 minutes E . Add the powdered sugar and vanilla and continue whisking on low until stiff peaks form, about 1 minute more. Scoop half of the whipped cream into a separate medium bowl and whisk in the cocoa powder until just combined. Scoop alternating spoonfuls of vanilla and chocolate whipped cream into the pit of the cake F . Use a butter knife to swirl together in a twist pattern. Use a vegetable peeler to peel ribbons of chocolate from the reserved chocolate bar onto the top of the whipped cream.

LIFE SKILL

To separate an egg, crack it open and hold one hand over a small bowl. Gently drop the egg into your hand, letting the white slip through your fingers while the yolk stays put. Place the yolk in a separate bowl.

easy fried ice cream

3 cups **puffed rice cereal**, such as Rice Krispies

4 tablespoons (½ stick) **unsalted butter**

1 teaspoon **ground cinnamon**

2 pints **ice cream**, any flavor

Honey, **caramel sauce**, **hot fudge**, **whipped cream**, **cinnamon sugar**, for topping (optional)

Fried ice cream sounds like a total contradiction, but skipping the deep-fryer makes this dessert seem almost logical. (Adulting isn't just about breaking the rules, it's also about *improving* them.) Crushed cereal, toasted in butter and cinnamon, makes for a perfect crunchy coating and from there the finishing touches are limitless. Get creative with toppings or, even better, make a toppings bar and let everyone design their own sundae.

1 Using a large ziptop bag and rolling pin, or 4 to 5 pulses in a food processor, crush the cereal into small pieces. Melt the butter in a large skillet over medium heat. Add the cinnamon and cereal and toss to coat. Cook for about 5 minutes, stirring occasionally, until warmed through and golden. Pour the cereal into a wide, shallow bowl or pie pan and let cool completely.

2 Cut the ice cream pints in half in their containers and quickly squeeze the ice cream into 4 balls, like you're making a snowball. Roll the balls through the cereal mixture, scooping and pressing to cover the ice cream completely, and place on a rimmed baking sheet. Freeze for at least 15 minutes. Serve with any variety of toppings.

citrus olive oil cake

Nonstick cooking spray
1½ cups **all-purpose flour**
1 cup **granulated sugar**
½ teaspoon **baking soda**
½ teaspoon **baking powder**
¼ teaspoon **kosher salt**
2 large **eggs**
½ cup plain **Greek yogurt**
2 teaspoons **orange zest**
¼ cup **fresh orange juice**
½ cup **olive oil**
½ cup **powdered sugar**
1 tablespoon **lemon zest**
2 tablespoons **fresh lemon juice**

A double dose of citrus makes this cake a surprisingly refreshing end to any meal. The recipe calls for orange and lemon, but truthfully, any acidic fruit would be excellent. Lime, grapefruit, blood orange, Meyer lemon—choose whatever looks best at the moment. A heavy pour of olive oil makes for a moist crumb and a rich base that's begging to be cut with the brightness of something tart. Don't have a loaf pan? Use an 8 by 8-inch baking pan instead.

1 Set a rack in the center of the oven and preheat to 350°F. Lightly coat a 9 by 5-inch loaf pan with nonstick spray and set it on a rimmed baking sheet.

2 In a large bowl, whisk together the flour, sugar, baking soda, baking powder, and salt. Add the eggs, yogurt, orange zest and juice, and olive oil and whisk again until just combined. Pour the batter into the prepared pan and transfer, along with the baking sheet, to the oven. Bake for 45 to 50 minutes, until a toothpick inserted into the center comes out clean.

3 Set the loaf pan on a wire rack on the baking sheet to cool for about 10 minutes. In a small bowl, whisk together the powdered sugar and lemon zest and juice. Turn the cake out and place it on top of the wire rack. Spoon the lemon icing over the warm cake, letting some drip down the sides and some soak into the top. Cool completely before slicing.

homemade hot chocolate

1 cup **whole milk**

2½ tablespoons **unsweetened cocoa powder**

1½ tablespoons **sugar**

Pinch of **ground cinnamon**

Pinch of **kosher salt**

Pinch of **cayenne pepper** (optional)

Whipped cream and **chocolate shavings**, for topping (optional)

A mug of hot chocolate is such an achievable luxury at the end of the day. (Or the start of the day, tbh.) Make one at a time or batch it up so it's ready all winter long. The recipe calls for whipped cream because this book is called *Adulting*, but if your heart still yearns for mini marshmallows, just know you are beautiful and more than enough. The adulting part is being able to comfort yourself.

1 Microwave the milk in a microwave-safe mug for 1 to 2 minutes, in 30-second intervals, until it's hot. Add the cocoa, sugar, cinnamon, salt, and cayenne (if using) and stir well.

2 Before serving, top with whipped cream and chocolate shavings, if desired.

BATCH OF MIX

MAKES 20 MUGS

3 cups **unsweetened cocoa powder**

2 cups **sugar**

1 tablespoon **ground cinnamon**

1 tablespoon **kosher salt**

1 Add the cocoa, sugar, cinnamon, and salt to a large ziptop bag or plastic storage container. Seal tightly and shake well to combine.

2 Use ¼ cup of this mix in place of the cocoa, sugar, cinnamon, salt in the master recipe. Store the mix in a cool, dry place for up to 6 months.

LIFE SKILL

Parchment paper helps extra sticky cakes, like this one, slide right out of the pan. It also saves you a lot of frustration when it comes to washing dishes!

caramel-apple
upside-down cake

Nonstick cooking spray

FOR THE CARAMEL

1 cup (packed) **light brown sugar**

4 tablespoons (½ stick) **unsalted butter**

1 teaspoon **vanilla extract**

1 teaspoon **ground cinnamon**

¼ cup chopped **raw pecans**

1 **apple**, peeled, cored, and sliced ½ inch thick

FOR THE CAKE

1¾ cups **all-purpose flour**

¾ teaspoon **baking powder**

¼ teaspoon **baking soda**

2 teaspoons **ground cinnamon**

1 teaspoon **kosher salt**

¼ teaspoon **ground nutmeg**

1 stick **unsalted butter**, at room temperature

1 cup **granulated sugar**

½ cup (packed) **light brown sugar**

2 large **eggs**

1 teaspoon **vanilla extract**

½ cup **milk**

¼ cup **apple cider**

Flaky sea salt, for topping

Vanilla ice cream, for serving

All respect to the classic pineapple upside-downer, but this cake will take it from here, thanks. Salted caramel, pecans, and apple slices cover a fluffy, richly spiced cider cake. Serve warm, with a generous scoop of ice cream. Did you already forget about pineapple? Exactly.

1 Set a rack in the center of the oven and preheat to 350°F. Trace the bottom of a 9-inch round cake pan on parchment and cut it out. Lightly coat the cake pan with nonstick spray. Set the parchment in the bottom and coat with more spray. Set the cake pan on a rimmed baking sheet.

2 Make the caramel: Combine the brown sugar, butter, vanilla, and cinnamon in a small saucepan over medium heat. Cook, stirring often, until bubbles just begin to rise, 3 to 4 minutes. Pour the caramel into the cake pan. Sprinkle the pecans on top, then arrange the apple slices in a circular pattern, gently pressing them into the caramel.

3 Make the cake: Whisk the flour, baking powder, baking soda, cinnamon, salt, and nutmeg in a large bowl. In a separate medium bowl, use an electric mixer on medium to whisk the butter and two sugars together until soft and fluffy, 2 to 3 minutes. Add the eggs and vanilla and continue whisking on medium to combine, about 1 minute more. Add the milk and apple cider and whisk again until fully incorporated, about 1 more minute.

4 Whisk half of the flour mixture into the wet mixture until mostly combined. Add the remaining flour mixture and use a spatula to fold together until a cohesive batter forms.

5 Pour the batter over the caramel in the cake pan and transfer, along with the baking sheet, to the oven. Bake for 60 to 65 minutes, until a toothpick inserted into the center comes out clean. Run a knife around the edge of the pan, place a serving plate over the cake pan, and immediately flip. Gently tap the bottom of the pan to release the cake onto the plate. Carefully lift the pan off and peel away the parchment. Top with flaky sea salt and allow the cake to cool for 20 minutes before slicing and serving with ice cream.

millionaire's pie

Nonstick cooking spray

FOR THE CRUST

1¾ cups **all-purpose flour**

6 tablespoons **sugar**

½ teaspoon **kosher salt**

1½ sticks **unsalted butter**, melted

FOR THE CARAMEL

2 (11-ounce) bags of **soft caramel candies**, such as Kraft Caramels

½ cup **heavy cream**

FOR THE CHOCOLATE

3 (3-ounce) bars **semisweet chocolate**, chopped

1 cup **heavy cream**

Flaky sea salt, for topping

Traditionally baked into a bar, Millionaire's Shortbread is a cookie crust with caramel filling and chocolate on top. If that sounds like a certain candy bar with two sticks, you're on the right track. Now, in pie form, the richness (millionaire, get it?) is off the charts. A shortbread crust houses a literal pool of soft caramel and a spread of salted chocolate ganache covers it all. It's the ultimate dessert to serve when you want to feel like a million bucks.

1 Set a rack in the center of the oven and preheat to 350°F. Lightly coat a 9-inch deep-dish pie pan with nonstick spray.

2 Make the crust: Whisk together the flour, sugar, and salt in a medium bowl. Pour in the melted butter and use clean hands to squeeze until a sandy dough comes together. Working in handfuls, scoop the dough into the pie pan, pressing into an even crust before adding more. The crust should cover the bottom and sides of the pie pan in an even layer. Use a fork to pierce holes along the bottom and sides of the crust. Transfer to the oven and bake for about 30 minutes, until lightly golden all over. Let the crust cool on a wire rack for about 30 minutes.

3 Make the caramel: Combine the caramel candies and cream in a medium saucepan over low heat. Cook, stirring occasionally, until completely melted, about 5 minutes. Pour the caramel sauce into the crust. Loosely cover with plastic wrap and refrigerate for about 30 minutes.

4 Make the chocolate: Place the chopped chocolate in a small bowl. Heat the cream in a small saucepan over medium heat until it just begins to boil. Pour the cream over the chocolate and let it sit undisturbed for 10 minutes. Whisk the chocolate and cream together until a cohesive, slightly fluffy mixture forms. Pour the chocolate over the caramel in the pie pan and sprinkle with flaky sea salt. Loosely cover with plastic wrap and refrigerate for at least 30 minutes, until the chocolate has set, or up to 24 hours before serving.

rocky road candies

Nonstick cooking spray

1 (12-ounce) bag **semisweet chocolate chips**

2 tablespoons **unsalted butter**

1 (14-ounce) can **sweetened condensed milk**

2½ cups **dry-roasted peanuts**

1 (10-ounce) bag **mini marshmallows**

A no-bake recipe that takes under five minutes to assemble, these candies are the definition of can't stop won't stop. Your brain says you've had enough, but your hand still floats over to the plate. Do you fight it? When they're this delicious, why bother?

1   Lightly coat a 9 by 13-inch baking pan with nonstick spray. Lay a piece of parchment paper across the pan lengthwise, with a 2-inch overhang on either side. Lay another piece of parchment across the dish in the opposite direction, creating a cross, with a 2-inch overhang.

2   Combine the chocolate chips and butter in a large microwave-safe bowl. Microwave on high for 30-second intervals, using a spatula to stir in between each, until the mixture is melted and smooth, about 2 minutes total. Stir in the condensed milk. Use a spatula to fold in the peanuts and mini marshmallows.

3   Scrape the candy mixture into the prepared baking pan and press to form one smooth, even layer. Loosely cover with plastic wrap and chill in the refrigerator for at least 30 minutes, until the chocolate is set.

4   Use the parchment overhang to lift the candy out of the pan. Cut lengthwise into 3 long strips, then cut each strip into 8 candies, making 24 squares total.

LIFE SKILL

Fold means using a spatula to incorporate ingredients super gently. With a light touch, run the spatula across the bottom and up the side of the bowl, fold the mixture over itself, then drive the spatula to the bottom of the bowl to repeat the motion. Rotate the bowl as you fold for even mixing.

COMPANY'S COMING

A CHEESE PLATE DONE RIGHT

A cheese plate is a delight that never goes out of style. But at a certain point, a tray full of disorganized who-knows-what with stuff and things and some stale crackers just doesn't feel very adult.

To build the perfect grown-up cheese plate, just remember the old rhyme: "Something old, something new, something stinky, something blue." Well, that's not exactly how it goes, but the point is *variety*! Textural differences between soft, firm, and hard—plus a mix of cow, sheep, and goat cheeses—will guarantee a perfect platter. Aged Gouda, Manchego, or Parmesan (old) offer a balance to soft ricotta, Brie, or chèvre (new). Taleggio and Camembert (stinky) taste better than they smell, and Gorgonzola or Roquefort (blue) will round out your plate.

But you don't need to break the bank! Two ounces of cheese (total) per guest will be plenty.

When it comes to other accoutrements, less is more. Commit to either a sliced baguette or your favorite cracker, but not both. Similarly, stick with one type of nut. Toasted walnuts are great on a budget; Marcona almonds are there when you're feeling spendy. Hit a savory note with one cured meat, plus something acidic like grainy mustard or sour cornichon pickles. And finish with a sweet note like sliced stone fruit or a bowl of jam or honey.

For a beautiful arrangement, place your cheeses at 12, 3, 6, and 9 o'clock. Slice a couple pieces off of each cheese, then leave a few knives, so guests can serve themselves and not be afraid to go first. Set any bowls of condiments at the outer corners. Spread pockets of nuts, meat, and fruit along the sides and in the spaces. Bread or crackers can surround the cheese if the board is large enough or go on a separate plate alongside. Give it all plenty of room to breathe—you want a platter that looks bountiful but not overloaded.

classic shrimp cocktail

FOR THE SHRIMP

2 cups **ice**

4 **garlic cloves**, smashed

4 sprigs **fresh parsley**

1 medium **white onion**, halved

1 tablespoon **kosher salt**

1 **lemon**, halved

1 pound **jumbo shrimp**, peeled
and deveined

FOR THE COCKTAIL SAUCE

½ cup **ketchup**

1 tablespoon prepared
horseradish

1 tablespoon **fresh lemon juice**

1 teaspoon **Worcestershire
sauce**

1 teaspoon **hot sauce**

Classic and classy, shrimp cocktail is the prime example of champagne taste on a beer budget. The only real investment you need to make is the shrimp, which can be acquired at high quality for not-high prices in the freezer section. Just remember to move it to the refrigerator twelve to twenty-four hours before you're ready to use it. Everything else might already be in your refrigerator. Sure, you could buy this, but when you make it yourself, you'll feel *very* adult.

1 Make the shrimp: Prepare a large bowl with 6 cups of water and the ice. Set aside. Add 6 cups of water plus the garlic, parsley, onion, and salt to a large saucepan over high heat. Squeeze the lemon halves into the water and bring to a boil. Remove the pan from the heat and add the shrimp. Poach for 4 minutes, until the shrimp are just opaque. Immediately remove the shrimp to the ice bath using a spider or slotted spoon. Let cool completely, about 10 minutes, then transfer the shrimp to paper towels to drain. Dry thoroughly and arrange in a serving dish.

2 Make the cocktail sauce: Mix the ketchup, horseradish, lemon juice, Worcestershire, and hot sauce together in a small bowl. Transfer to a serving bowl alongside the prepared shrimp.

buffalo chicken dip

FOR THE DIP

¼ cup diced **carrot**

¼ cup diced **celery**

1 (8-ounce) package **cream cheese**, at room temperature

¼ cup crumbled **blue cheese**

2 tablespoons **hot sauce**

1 tablespoon **chicken broth** (see page 46) or store-bought **chicken stock**

1 teaspoon **onion powder**

1 teaspoon **garlic powder**

FOR THE CHICKEN

2 tablespoons plain **bread crumbs**

2 tablespoons grated **Parmesan cheese**

2 tablespoons **all-purpose flour**

2 tablespoons **cornstarch**

½ teaspoon plus a pinch of **kosher salt**

½ teaspoon **freshly ground black pepper**

1 large **egg**

½ cup **olive oil**

½ pound boneless, skinless **chicken breast**, cut into ½-inch cubes

Sturdy **crackers** or thinly sliced and toasted **baguette**, for serving

Creamy, crunchy, tangy, spicy. Oh, and we aren't even talking about the fried chicken on top. This dip has all the pleasures of a plate of wings without necessitating wet wipes or sauce mouth. Veggies, blue cheese, hot sauce, and chicken all in one perfect bite! It's like a football Sunday, but more delicious.

1 Make the dip: Reserve 1 tablespoon each of the carrot and celery. Mix the remaining carrot and celery along with the cream cheese, blue cheese, hot sauce, chicken broth, onion powder, and garlic powder in a medium bowl.

2 Make the chicken: Combine the bread crumbs, Parmesan, flour, cornstarch, ½ teaspoon salt, and pepper in a medium bowl. In a small bowl, whisk the egg with the pinch of salt.

3 Heat the olive oil in a large saucepan over medium-high heat. Drop a small pinch of the bread crumb mixture into the oil; it should sizzle immediately. Working in batches, dip a quarter of the chicken into the egg mixture, allowing any excess to drip off, then dredge in the bread crumbs, and carefully drop into the oil. Fry for 3 to 4 minutes, until the coating is deep brown and crispy. Remove the chicken to a paper towel–lined plate to drain. Repeat with the remaining chicken.

4 Reserve a quarter of the fried chicken. Fold the remaining chicken into the dip. Transfer to a serving bowl and top with the reserved carrot, celery, and fried chicken. Serve immediately with a spoon and crackers.

guacamole glow up

THE CLASSIC

¼ medium **white onion**, finely chopped

1 **jalapeño**, seeded and finely chopped

1 **garlic clove**, finely chopped

¼ cup **fresh cilantro leaves**, finely chopped

1 teaspoon **kosher salt**, plus more as needed

4 large ripe **Hass avocados**

Juice of 1 **lime**, plus more as needed

There are three things you need to remember for a great batch of guacamole every time. First, don't bother with the tomatoes. They just drag everything down. Second, chop your flavoring ingredients as finely as possible. A mortar and pestle or a quick whirl in a food processor are helpful, but good old-fashioned elbow grease works, too. And finally, keep a good mash-to-chunk ratio among the avocados: mostly smooth with some big pieces, all coated in flavoring mixture. The classic dip is excellent on its own, but the sweet and savory glow ups that follow are always a great idea.

1   Use a wooden spoon (or mortar and pestle) to mix together the onion, jalapeño, garlic, cilantro, and salt in a medium bowl. Press the mixture hard on the sides of the bowl to slightly mash and open up the flavors.

2   Halve the avocados, remove the pits, and scoop the flesh into the bowl. Use the wooden spoon to break up and lightly mash the avocados, creating a variety of textures from smooth to large chunks. Add the lime juice and stir everything together. Taste for seasoning and add more salt or lime as needed.

ELOTE

1 tablespoon **olive oil**

½ cup **frozen corn**, thawed

½ cup crumbled **Cotija cheese**

1 recipe **The Classic** guacamole (see above)

1 teaspoon **chili powder**

1   Heat the oil in a medium skillet over medium-high heat. When the oil is shimmering, add the corn and cook, stirring occasionally, for about 10 minutes, until charred and tender.

2   Set aside 2 tablespoons of the corn and 2 tablespoons of Cotija. Fold the remaining corn and Cotija into the classic guacamole. Sprinkle the reserved corn and Cotija on top, finishing with the chili powder, and serve.

TROPICAL

½ cup **pomegranate seeds**

½ cup diced **mango**

1 recipe **The Classic** guacamole (see above)

1   Reserve 2 tablespoons of the pomegranate seeds. Fold the remaining seeds and all of the mango pieces into the classic guacamole.

2   Sprinkle the reserved pomegranate seeds over the top and serve.

2-ingredient-dough pizza

THE DOUGH

1½ cups **self-rising flour**,
plus more for dusting

1 cup plain **Greek yogurt**

Two ingredients and no rise time. You'll be asking yourself, "Can an adult eat pizza for every meal?" The answer is . . . not no. More specifically, can an adult pull a fresh pizza out of the oven every time company comes over? With five delicious treatments, that answer is a hard and undeniable yes.

1 Set a rack in the center of the oven and preheat to 400°F. Line a rimmed baking sheet with parchment paper.

2 In a large bowl, use a wooden spoon to mix together the flour and yogurt A until a cohesive dough forms B . (Add more flour 1 tablespoon at a time if the dough is too sticky.) Turn the dough out onto a floured work surface. Knead it for about 1 minute to achieve a smooth ball of dough C . Use a rolling pin to roll the dough into a 12-inch round, about ¼ inch thick D . If the dough sticks, sprinkle a little more flour over it. Carefully lift the dough onto the prepared baking sheet.

3 Choose your desired pizza and proceed as directed.

SALAD ON PIZZA

¼ cup **olive oil**

2 **garlic cloves**, smashed

5 thin slices **prosciutto**

1 cup **arugula**

¼ medium **red onion**,
thinly sliced

½ **lemon**

2 ounces **Parmesan cheese**

1 Heat the olive oil and garlic in a small saucepan over low heat for about 10 minutes, until the garlic just begins to sizzle, but not brown. Remove from the heat and discard the garlic. Reserve 1 tablespoon of the garlic oil and set aside.

2 Brush the prepared pizza dough with the garlic oil from the pan. Arrange the prosciutto across the top. Bake for about 15 minutes, until the dough is browned and the prosciutto is crisp.

3 Combine the arugula and onion in a medium bowl and squeeze in the lemon. Toss together and sprinkle over the baked pizza. Use a vegetable peeler to grate ribbons of Parmesan over the top. Drizzle the reserved tablespoon of garlic oil over the pizza.

4 Cut the pizza into 8 slices and serve immediately.

LEMON RICOTTA

2 tablespoons **olive oil**

3 **garlic cloves**, thinly sliced

6 tablespoons **ricotta cheese**

½ **lemon**, thinly sliced

¼ cup grated **Parmesan**

Zest of ½ **lemon**

½ teaspoon **red pepper flakes**

Freshly ground black pepper

1 Brush the prepared pizza dough with the oil. Sprinkle the garlic, drop the ricotta by the spoonful, and lay the lemon slices around the dough. Bake for about 20 minutes, until the dough, ricotta, and lemon are starting to brown.

2 Sprinkle the Parmesan, lemon zest, and red pepper flakes on top of the pizza. Season generously with black pepper.

3 Cut the pizza into 8 slices and serve immediately.

HOLY PEPPERONI

½ cup **pizza sauce**

1 cup shredded **mozzarella**

¼ medium **green bell pepper**, sliced

¼ medium **red onion**, sliced

12 to 16 **pepperoni slices**

1 Spread the pizza sauce, mozzarella, pepper, onion, and pepperoni over the prepared dough. Bake for about 20 minutes, until the dough is browned and the pepperoni is crisp.

2 Cut the pizza into 8 slices and serve immediately.

SLICE SHOP MOZZ

½ cup **pizza sauce**

1 cup shredded **mozzarella**

½ teaspoon **dried oregano**

½ teaspoon **garlic powder**

½ teaspoon grated **Parmesan**

½ teaspoon **red pepper flakes**

1 Spread the pizza sauce and mozzarella over the prepared dough. Bake for about 20 minutes, until the dough is browned and the cheese is melted. Mix the oregano, garlic powder, Parmesan, and red pepper flakes in a small bowl then sprinkle over the top.

2 Cut the pizza into 8 slices and serve immediately.

FENNEL & SAUSAGE

1 tablespoon **olive oil**

2 **spicy Italian sausages**, casings removed

½ cup **pizza sauce**

1 cup shredded **mozzarella**

¼ **fennel bulb**, thinly sliced

1 tablespoon **fennel fronds**

1 Heat the oil in a medium skillet over medium heat. When the oil is shimmering, add the sausages and cook, using a wooden spoon to break them up and stir occasionally, for about 10 minutes, until cooked through.

2 Spread the pizza sauce over the prepared dough. Cover in mozzarella and the fennel slices. Top with the sausage and oil from the skillet. Bake for about 20 minutes, until the dough is browned and the cheese is fully melted. Sprinkle the fennel fronds over the top.

3 Cut the pizza into 8 slices and serve immediately.

sheet pan
nachos al pastor

1 tablespoon **olive oil**

1 pound **boneless pork chop**

Kosher salt and **freshly ground black pepper**

8 slices **white American cheese**

1 (4-ounce) can **diced green chiles**

¼ cup **whole milk**

½ (7-ounce) can **chipotles in adobo**

1 (8-ounce) can **crushed pineapple**

1 **garlic clove**, crushed

½ tablespoon **dried oregano**

1 teaspoon **ground cumin**

1 (12-ounce) bag **tortilla chips**

1 (15.5-ounce) can **pinto beans**, drained and rinsed

4 **radishes**, thinly sliced

2 **scallions**, thinly sliced

½ cup **fresh cilantro leaves**, coarsely chopped

Traditionally *al pastor* (aka delicious Mexican pork) is cooked on a spit for hours and then sliced to order. But after a quick char in the pan and an equally quick simmer in a spicy-sweet sauce, no one will know you took a genius shortcut. Spooned over warm tortilla chips, covered in a gooey cheese sauce, and finished with crunchy toppings, the al pastor in these nachos guarantees a no-leftovers dish. For the illusion of effortless hosting, prepare the al pastor and cheese sauce ahead of time; gently reheat them while the chips and beans bake.

1 Set a rack in the center of the oven and preheat to 400°F.

2 Heat the oil in a grill pan or medium skillet over medium-high heat. Generously season the pork chop on both sides with salt and pepper. Place in the grill pan and sear for about 7 minutes, until the bottom is charred in places. Flip and grill the other side for about 7 minutes more, until the pork is cooked through. Remove the pork to a clean cutting board and let rest for 10 minutes.

3 Meanwhile, combine the American cheese, green chiles, and milk in a small saucepan over medium-low heat. Cook, stirring occasionally, until the cheese has completely melted to form a cohesive sauce, about 5 minutes. Reduce the heat to the lowest setting to keep warm.

4 Slice the pork lengthwise into ¼-inch-thick ribbons, then coarsely chop into 1- to 2-inch pieces. Place the pork, chipotles, pineapple, garlic, oregano, cumin, salt, pepper, and ½ cup of water in a medium saucepan over medium heat. Simmer, stirring occasionally, until the pork is coated in a thick sauce and most of the liquid has cooked off, 10 to 12 minutes.

5 Meanwhile, arrange the chips on a rimmed baking sheet and scatter the pinto beans on top. Bake for 10 minutes, until the chips are slightly toasted and the beans are slightly dried and cracked. Spoon the pork mixture over the top, then drizzle the cheese sauce over everything. Finish with a shower of radishes, scallions, and cilantro.

ACKNOWLEDGMENTS

Original Recipe Developer

Casey Elsass

Contributing Producers

Betsy Carter

Joey Firoben

Rachel Gaewski

Crystal Hatch

Jordan Kenna

Gwenaelle Le Cochennec

Evelyn Liu

Rie McClenny

Nathan Ng

Claire Nolan

Merle O'Neal

Tayo Ola

Alexander Roberts

Teddy Villa

Everyone at Tasty

Emily DePaula

Talia Halperin

Angela Krasnick

Jailyn Paulino

Parker Ortolani

Ines Pacheco

Eric Karp

Bill Guy

And the entire Tasty &
BuzzFeed team

Everyone at Clarkson Potter

Amanda Englander

Lily Ertischek

Stephanie Huntwork

Jen Wang

Derek Gullino

Kim Tyner

Mark McCauslin

Merri Ann Morrell

Kate Tyler

David Hawk

Windy Dorresteyn

Stephanie Davis

Andrea Portanova

Aaron Wehner

Doris Cooper

Jill Flaxman

Styling and Photography

Lauren Volo

Monica Pierini

Maeve Sheridan

Christina Zhang

Krystal Rack

Andie McMahon

INDEX

10 9 8 7 6 5 4 3 2 1

Ebury Press, an imprint of Ebury Publishing
20 Vauxhall Bridge Road
London SW1V 2SA

Ebury Press is part of the Penguin Random House
group of companies whose addresses can be found at
global.penguinrandomhouse.com

First published in the US by Clarkson Potter 2020
This edition published in the UK by Ebury Press 2020

www.penguin.co.uk

A CIP catalogue record for this book is available from
the British Library

Book and cover design by Jen Wang
Cover photograph by Lauren Volo

ISBN 9781785039461

Printed and bound in Italy by L.E.G.O. S.p.A

Penguin Random House is committed to a sustainable
future for our business, our readers and our planet.
This book is made from Forest Stewardship Council®
certified paper.